How to Sew with Confidence

Master the essential sewing techniques with **10 practical projects** to inspire you

Margo Price

Publishing and Legal Notices

Copyright

Liability

We have used our best efforts to ensure that the content of this document is both useful and correct at the time of publication. The content of this document is supplied for information only and is subject to change without notice. The authors assume no responsibility or liability for any errors or inaccuracies that may appear in this document, nor the use to which it may be put.

This document is for information only and does not represent a legal contract or agreement.

Publishing Information

Author:	Margo Price
	www.time4me-workshops.co.uk
Editor/Designer:	Andrew A Moore
Published By:	AAM Design Limited
	www.aamdesign.co.uk
Publication Number:	T4M-002
Issue Number:	1
Issue Date:	October 2013

About this Document

This document describes practical sewing projects and basic techniques for beginner and intermediate sewing machine users.

Contents

Part 1: Introduction

Learning to sew is practical, educational and fun.

Welcome

In this book, I have put together a collection of simple and practical projects to enable you master essential basic sewing techniques and get the best from your sewing machine.

About Margo Price

Since I was a child, I have loved nothing better than working with fabric and yarn. My mother was a keen seamstress and knitter and we spent many happy hours making clothes for my dolls. She even helped me to knit a school jumper on her ancient Turmix knitting machine, which I then proceeded to unravel and reknit three times in one term! Since 2001, I have been running workshops in sewing and other crafts from my home in in Hampshire on the South coast of England.

My aim is to help promote traditional sewing and needlecrafts and pass on my knowledge, skills and experience to those who would like to learn, or perhaps already enjoy, sewing, knitting, and other such activities.

In this book you will find practical advice and help that will make your sewing projects easier and, hopefully, more enjoyable too.

If you find this book useful and inspiring please let me know, either through my website, www.time4me-workshops.co.uk, or my facebook page www.facebook.com/pages/Handmade-by-Margo. Similarly, if you have any questions or problems then I'd like to hear about that too.

Margo Price

Margo Price has a BA in 3D Design from Portsmouth University specialising in textiles and an MA in Creative Writing from the University of Chichester.

She has over 30-years experience of sewing and knitting, including running a party-plan knitwear business and a sewing tuition business.

Margo is a contributor to *Sewing World* magazine and other craft-related publications. She is also the author of "*How to Make a Living from Crafts*".

She has had exhibitions of her handbags, knitted from enamelled wire, at the Beatrice Royal Gallery, the Littlehampton Museum and the Top Drawer fair at Earl's Court.

Learning to Sew

Learning to sew can be difficult without a good teacher and not everyone has the benefit of skills handed down from a family member or friend. If you are a beginner, this book is a good place to start. I will help you master the basic techniques required for many different sewing projects and, hopefully, guide you towards more advanced ones.

How Will I Learn?

I believe the best way to learn how to sew, as with many other things, is to get stuck into a project and make something. We start off with a few helpful tips on buying and getting started on a sewing machine, which threads to use and a list of the only sewing notions you will need. This is followed by a selection of simple projects which gradually get more complex and introduce you to more advanced techniques.

The techniques, required for each project, are explained in the back half of the book, so you can simply refer to them as you need them. This ensures that you don't have to wade through a lot of theory before you start making things.

By the time you reach the end of the book you will, hopefully, have completed all the projects, learned all the techniques and feel ready to tackle more advanced projects.

What's in this Book?

This book contains basic projects for practical household items and accessories that I have developed and taught in my classes and workshops.

Part 1: Introduction

Part 1 provides an introduction to the teaching methods I will be using throughout this book. It also explains how this book is structured and explains the fundamentals of using a sewing machine.

Part 2: Simple Sewing Projects

Part 2 contains all the sewing projects, starting with the simplest and gradually moving towards the most complex.

The instructions are concisely written to allow those of you with some sewing skills and knowledge to proceed quickly through each step.

Each project refers to the techniques you will need in order to complete it. These are located in Part 3 of this book (links are provided for PDF / e-book / online readers).

Technique: Binding Edges   >

Videos, and other sewing tips, can be viewed on my website at (www.time4me-workshops.co.uk/tips.htm).

Part 3: Basic Sewing Techniques

Part 3 details the techniques you will need in order to make the projects. Again, these are described in order of complexity. So you can read them all in sequence, if you feel that would work better for you. I recommend, however, that you read them, as you need them, to avoid feeling overwhelmed by all the information.

Part 4: What Next?

Part 4 describes other related books and websites where you can find more inspiration and advice to help you become more skilful with your sewing machine.

Sewing Machine Basics

This section is an introduction to buying and learning to use your sewing machine. As each sewing machine is slightly different, you will have to read the manual for your particular model to learn how to use all its functions and features.

Buying a Sewing Machine

Buying a sewing machine is an important occasion. There are so many different makes and models out there which do all sorts of different things. Knowing which to choose can be quite a challenge. If you're thinking of buying a new or second-hand sewing machine, here are a few essential tips to ensure that get the machine you really need.

Make a List of the Features you Want

Before you go anywhere near a sewing machine dealer, think very carefully about all the projects that you're ever likely to want to tackle. Make a list to take along with you to the dealer.

Research Your Local Dealers

Ask sewing friends or tutors for details of any reputable sewing machine dealers in your area. Only buy from a dealer that will offer you help and instruction on your chosen machine before and after you've bought it.

Buy From a Reputable Dealer

Supermarkets, catalogue stores, shopping channels or newspaper ads will not be able to give you any advice on what you need. Once you've paid your money you're on your own.

Choose a Machine with Separate Stitch-width / Stitch-length Controls

There are a number of budget sewing machines on the market that have many fancy built-in stitches but no separate stitch adjustment controls. You will soon find that these are of limited use. A sewing machine that has separate stitch width and stitch length controls can open up a whole world of possibilities by allowing you to change existing built-in stitches into something completely new.

Choose a Sewing Machine with the Facility to Drop the Feed Dogs

Choose a sewing machine that has a drop-feed facility (where the feed dogs can be lowered out of use) and avoid those that come supplied with a plastic plate to cover the permanently raised feed dogs. You can only do proper machine embroidery with a drop-feed facility.

Check-Out both New & Second-Hand Machines

Ask your dealer to show you his range of new and second-hand sewing machines. You may be able to pick up a good robust second-hand model that has all the basic features you need, for the price of a newer, flimsier one.

Check Which Presser Feet Are Included

Generally, new machines have fewer extras than older, second-hand ones. You will need:

- a standard zig-zag foot.
- a zipper foot.
- a buttonhole foot.
- a darning or open-toed embroidery foot (compulsory for machine embroidery but you may need to buy it separately).

Check Which Thread Reel Sizes Can Be Used

Choose a sewing machine that will take all sizes of thread reels. Machines with self-threading cartridges may look inviting and easy to use but they're a real pain when the thread you want is on an awkwardly sized reel, which will not fit in the cartridge.

Choose a Front or Vertical Loading Bobbin for Machine Embroidery

If you want to try machine embroidery (and you will when you see just what you can do) choose a machine with a front-loading rather than a drop-in bobbin. These are more robust, easier for adjusting bobbin tension and much easier to dismantle for cleaning and snarl-ups.

Choose a Robust Machine

Whatever machine you choose, make sure it is robust enough to cope with your sewing needs but light enough for you to manage. And remember, you will probably need a dust cover for those periods between sewing projects.

Getting to Know Your Sewing Machine

You've bought the machine of your dreams, got it home and unpacked the box. Now it's sitting there waiting for you to make the first move. What do you do?

Read the Manual

Before you do anything else – READ THE MANUAL – especially the sections on threading and winding the bobbin. Also, check that you have all the bits the book says you should have.

Practice Some Basics

Learn How to Thread Your Machine

Thread the machine top (spool) and bottom (bobbin) with a good quality polyester thread with a dark colour on the top and a lighter shade on the bottom. Threading really is the most important thing you need to know. Practise it until you can do it with your eyes shut.

Set the Default Stitch Settings

Set the stitch length control to 2.5 mm and the stitch width to 0. These are the usual settings for an all-purpose straight stitch.

Prepare a Practice Piece

Cut a large square of strong, white cotton or calico. Iron, fold in half and iron again. This will be your practice piece.

Practice Stitching Some Straight Lines

Line up the edge of your presser foot with the edge of the fabric. Sew a line of straight stitching keeping the foot lined up with the edge of the fabric all the way to the bottom. Repeat these

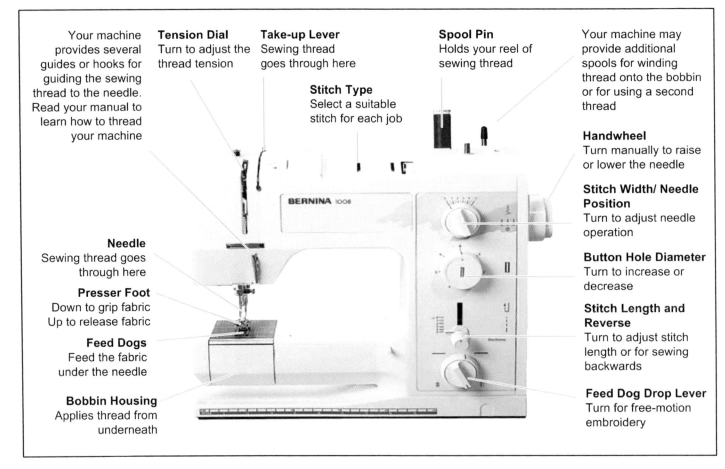

Your machine provides several guides or hooks for guiding the sewing thread to the needle. Read your manual to learn how to thread your machine

Tension Dial
Turn to adjust the thread tension

Take-up Lever
Sewing thread goes through here

Stitch Type
Select a suitable stitch for each job

Spool Pin
Holds your reel of sewing thread

Your machine may provide additional spools for winding thread onto the bobbin or for using a second thread

Handwheel
Turn manually to raise or lower the needle

Stitch Width/ Needle Position
Turn to adjust needle operation

Needle
Sewing thread goes through here

Presser Foot
Down to grip fabric
Up to release fabric

Feed Dogs
Feed the fabric under the needle

Bobbin Housing
Applies thread from underneath

Button Hole Diameter
Turn to increase or decrease

Stitch Length and Reverse
Turn to adjust stitch length or for sewing backwards

Feed Dog Drop Lever
Turn for free-motion embroidery

BERNINA 1006

lines of stitching, lining up the presser foot with the previous line of stitching until you have a collection of perfectly straight lines.

Check Your Tension

If you can see the bobbin thread on the top of your work, your top tension is too tight. If you can see the top thread on the reverse of your work, the bobbin tension is too tight.

If you have a machine with a top-loading bobbin, you will only be able to adjust the top tension. Experiment with this until your stitches look balanced, i.e. cannot see the bottom thread on top and vice versa.

Check Your Fabric Passes through the Machine Freely

Support the fabric. Hold it loosely in front of the needle bed with your right hand and loosely at the left of the needle bed with your left hand. Do not try to pull or push the fabric through the machine, just guide it gently. It is good practice to avoid putting your hands on the needle bed when the machine is in motion, both for safety reasons and to ensure that you're not tempted to push or pull the fabric.

Learn to Maintain a Steady Speed

An uneven and jerky speed will produce uneven and jerky stitching. You do not need to be going at full speed but going too slowly will make it difficult to keep your stitching straight. Try and keep your speed to about half the machine's full speed.

Tryout the Reverse Lever

When you have a line of straight stitches try the same thing again but start and finish each line with a few stitches using the reverse lever on your sewing machine.

Try Some Other Stitches

Experiment with the built-in stitches provided on your sewing machine. Try altering the stitch length and width controls on each stitch. Don't forget to keep your stitching straight.

Sewing Machine Needles

Here are a few tips regarding sewing machine needles. There are different types to suit different fabrics. Make sure you use an appropriate needle for the job you are doing.

Needle Basics

All needles have a number and this dictates their size and thickness. They are different and the numbers may not seem to correlate but they do – the higher the number the thicker the diameter of the shaft above the eye.

In Europe, the sizes range from 60 to 100. In America it is generally 7 to 16. In practice this means that a 7/60 needle will be the thinnest and smallest, ideal for sewing sheer and delicate fabrics. In contrast the 16/100 will be perfect for sewing heavyweight fabrics like denims.

A Bit About Needles

Use a New Needle for Every New Project

Sewing machine needles are one of the cheapest sewing accessories and one that can make the biggest difference to your finished project.

Always Buy the Correct Brand of Needle for Your Machine

Not all needles fit all sewing machines and your instruction book should tell you what to buy.

If Your Thread Keeps Breaking – Check for Burrs

If you have fitted a new needle but your thread is still shredding or breaking, check the eye for metal burrs. These are tiny shards of metal that have been left behind by the manufacturing process and they can be seen by holding the needle up to a bright light or under a magnifying glass. Many new needles are defective and the cheaper the brand the more likely they are to be unusable. All you can do is discard them and try again.

Use 'Universal' Needles for Most of your General Sewing Needs

Universal (or general purpose) needles are available in a wide range of sizes from 7/60 to 16/100, with the smaller size being suitable for very light and sheer fabrics and the largest being suitable for thick fabrics such as coating, suiting, furnishings and canvas.

Use a 'Ballpoint' Needle for Knit Fabrics such as T-Shirts

The rounded point, of a ballpoint needle, will separate and stitch in between the loosely-woven fibres rather than slicing through them and causing them to unravel.

Use a 'Stretch' Type Needle for Synthetic Knits and Silky Polyesters

They are particularly good for avoiding static build-up on silky fabrics.

Use a 'Jeans' Needle for Denim

Jeans needles have a very sharp point that will slice through the heavy fabric with ease. They are available in sizes 14 and 16. Choose depending on the thickness of your jeans.

Use a 'Leather' Needle for Leather, Suede and other Heavy Non-Woven Fabrics

The wedge-shaped point of a leather needle will penetrate non-woven leather or suede fabrics without causing splits and tearing.

Use 'Handicap' Needles for Easier Threading

These have a fine slit in the side of the needle eye and are threaded by sliding the thread down the side of the shank until it pops into the eye.

Use a Double or Triple Needle for Multi-Coloured Edging

If you want to create some subtle patterning on your project but your machine doesn't have any stitches you fancy, use a double or triple needle for parallel rows of stitching in different colours. You will need a machine that is capable of zig-zag so the throat plate has a hole that is wide enough for the needles. You can only do straight stitch with this type of needle.

Getting Started with Essential Tools & Sewing Notions

The market is full of exciting, new products that claim to be indispensable in your sewing box. But you really only need a few basic tools. Always choose the best quality products you can afford.

What are Sewing Notions?

Notions are all the things you use for sewing such as: needles, thread, buttons, zips, bias tape, lining materials, seam binding, etc. In other words, anything other than the material itself.

What Will I Need?

Scissors

Choose good quality, full-size dressmaking scissors with comfortable handles and strong stainless-steel blades. Even if you don't plan to do any dressmaking, you will get a cleaner cut in any fabric with large scissors.

A smaller pair of lace or machine embroidery scissors is also useful to keep next to your machine. The type with curved points are invaluable for reaching under the presser foot to snip off loose threads.

A Wide Tape Measure

If you buy one in a bright colour with large inch and centimetre markings, in either a 60 or 90 inch length, you won't spend half the day looking for it. Make sure it has metal-bound ends to prevent fraying.

Standard and Long Pins

Choose a pack of standard dressmaking pins and one of long, slim-shank, quilting pins with flat, colourful heads and you'll be ready for anything. There is a huge variety of pins available now but it is just not necessary to buy different pins for every different project.

Seam Ripper

Make sure it has a sharp point and blade and a close fitting cover which will slide onto the handle when the ripper is in use. Keep the ripper blade covered when not in use in case you inadvertently pick it up by the wrong end.

Tailor's Chalk

Choose a good quality tailor's chalk in a triangular 'cake' form... if you can find it. These last for ages and can be easily sharpened to an 'edge'. There are chalks available in pencil form but these wear down very quickly. The plastic holders with the slot-in chalk dust capsules are a nifty design but don't leave a very strong line. Try to stick to light or neutral colours as the darker blues and reds can be waxy and difficult to remove.

Pack of Needles

Choose a pack of good quality sewing needles (sharps) of varying lengths. There are 'easy-thread' needles available now with open eyes to slot the thread in but, unless you use a thimble these are very hard on the fingers.

Metal Thimble

These can take a bit of getting used to if you've never used one before but are invaluable for tough hand-sewing jobs.

Flexible Curve

Originally devised for dressmaking, this bendy, plastic ruler, with centimetre markings on both sides, is great for drawing all sorts of smooth curves.

Pincushion

Try and find one that has feet and is filled with sawdust rather than wadding as this won't roll around on your work table and the sawdust will help keep your pins sharp.

Yard/Metre Stick

Choose a solid, wooden yard or metre stick rather than one of those collapsible ones that carpenters seem to carry around. They're invaluable for measuring long lengths of fabric and curtains.

Know Your Threads

Here are some top tips on threads. Using the appropriate threads for your projects, and your sewing machine, will make life so much easier.

Thread Tips

Don't Use Cheap or Poor-Quality Thread

It does not make economic sense to spend hundreds – or even thousands – of pounds on a sewing machine and then try to save money with budget threads.

Don't Use Old Thread

Old threads can become flattened on the reel and cause all sorts of problems from noisy running to thread and needle breakage. If you have inherited some old reels of thread, keep them for hand sewing.

Use a Good-Quality, All-Purpose, Polyester Thread for Your General Sewing Needs

Good quality polyester threads are:

- Durable
- Strong
- Colourfast
- Keep their shape and recover well after stretching.

Use a 100% Cotton Quilting Thread when Attaching Buttons and Bindings

Cotton threads are:

- Soft
- Strong
- Adjust well to any shrinkage in the fabric

Think Before You Use Nylon Monofilament Thread

When using nylon monofilament thread be aware of the following:

- It is not heat resistant
- It is not colourfast and will yellow over time
- It will become brittle with laundering

Know Your Thread Weights

A 40w thread is labelled as such as 40 Kilometres weighs 1 kilogram. A thread labelled 30w would only have 30 kilometres in a kilogram, as it is a thicker thread.

> **Remember:**
> The lower the number, the thicker the thread and the more it will show on your work.

You Don't Have to Use the Same Thread in the Bobbin as on the Top

It is perfectly acceptable to use lightweight polyester (50w) in the bobbin while using a heavier weight decorative thread in the top. Indeed, some threads, such as rayon embroidery or cotton quilting threads are springy and may cause snagging if used in the bobbin.

Know Your Spool Types

If you buy a large spool of thread, which is wound onto a cone-shaped core and has a large hole in the base, you cannot use this on your machine's spool holder as it will not unwind correctly. Use a thread stand instead. These comprise of a flat, weighted, plastic base with a metal spindle in the centre and a taller spindle, with a hook at the top on one side. The thread cone is placed on the central spindle and the thread looped over the hook and then routed through your machine's normal threading path.

When Buying Metallic Thread...

Check for the following:

- **Uniform winding** – if a thread is poorly wound it is probably poor quality.
- **Uniform colour** – changes in colour may indicate that the winding tension is too high and the thread has become damaged.
- **Bruises or flat spots** – if the thread has been roughly handled it may be damaged.

Don't Use Adhesive Tape to Stop Threads Unwinding from their Reels

The adhesive will rub off onto the thread which will leave deposits on the tension disks of your machine and in the needle eye.

Part 2: Simple Sewing Projects

Sewing projects for every room of your home.

Simple Tote Bag

This bag is the simplest, and probably the most useful bag you will ever make. You can keep it plain, or decorate it with buttons, appliqué or embroidery.

What is Webbing?

Webbing is a strong fabric woven as a flat strip often used in place of rope or strapping. The name "webbing" comes from the meshed material frequently used in its construction, which resembles a web.

One inch wide webbing is the most common size but smaller and larger sizes are available.

Webbing, for use in sewing, is usually made from cotton, but nylon, polyester and polypropylene are available too.

All webbing will unravel if the ends are not secured or finished in some way. When cutting a length, it is advisable to wrap the area that will be cut in tape and cut through the tape so that some tape remains on each end. Cotton webbing will need to be secured with stitching.

You Will Need

- **2 fat quarters (50cm x 50cm) or 1/2m cotton fabric for the main body of the bag.**
- **2 fat quarters (50cm x 50cm) or 1/2m cotton fabric for the bag lining.**
- **1 ¼ yds (1m) of 1" (2.5cm) wide webbing for the short handles – or 2 ½ yds (2m) for shoulder bag handles.**
- **Pins.**
- **All-purpose polyester thread.**

Hand-Dyed Fabrics
A range of hand-dyed cotton fabrics are available from www.time4me-workshops.co.uk/shop.

Machine Setup

All seam allowances are ¼" (1cm) unless stated otherwise.

A 2.5mm stitch length is used throughout except for the addition of appliqué images.

A standard zig-zag foot is used throughout.

To Make Your Bag

Cut Out Your Fabric

1   Iron your fabric and lay it out on a large level surface.

2   On the main body fabric, using tailor's chalk, mark 2 x rectangles 15" x 13".

3   On the lining fabric, using tailor's chalk, mark 2 x rectangles 15" x 13".

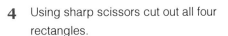

Technique: Accurate Measuring   >

4   Using sharp scissors cut out all four rectangles.

5   Cut your webbing strip in half so you have two pieces the same length.

6   Now lay one of the main fabric pieces, right side up on a flat surface. This will be your front panel.

Note:
It is not necessary to add any decoration to the bag but if you are planning to add an appliqué image or programmed embroidery to your bag front, it is a good idea to do it now. Buttons or hand embroidery can be added at the end.

7   On the top edge of the front panel, mark a point 2" in from each side edge.

8   Place the handles as shown in the diagram, lining up the edges of the webbing with the

2" marks and making sure that the handle is not twisted.

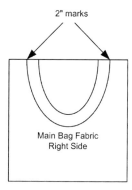

9 Repeat for the back panel and stitch both handle pieces in place, 1/4" from the top edge, using a 4mm straight stitch.

Assemble the Bag

10 Take one lining piece and place it face down on the front of the bag so the top edges are aligned.

11 Pin along the top edge ensuring that the raw edges of the handles are secured.

12 Using a straight stitch, stitch across the top edge ½" from the edge. Press seam open.

13 Repeat with the back panel.

14 Open out both panels and press the seam allowance open.

15 Now lay the front panel and the attached lining, on a flat surface, face up with the lining opened out.

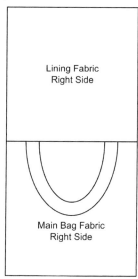

16 Lay the back panel and attached lining on top face down. Ensure that the handles are not going to get caught in the seams.

17 Pin all the way round, leaving a gap of about 8" in the bottom edge of the lining for turning. Ensure the seams joining the lining to the bag are accurately matched up.

18 Starting at one side of the 8" gap, stitch all the way round, ½" from the edge and using a 2.5mm stitch length, leaving the 8" gap open.

19 Trim the corners of the seam allowances, close to the stitching.

20 Turn bag right way out, through the 8" gap, and push out corners.

21 Turn in seam allowance in turning gap, pin, and, using a 2.5mm straight stitch, stitch close to the folded edge to close the gap.

Note:
If you would like your bag to be reversible, close the gap with neat hand-stitching rather than with the sewing machine. That way, the seam will lie flat when the bag is turned inside out.

22 Push lining into bag, pushing it right into the corners.

23 Press around top of bag ensuring seam is right on the edge.

24 Place a few pins around the top edge to stop the lining shifting when top-stitching.

25 Using a 3mm straight stitch, top-stitch all the way round the top of the bag ¼" from the edge.

26 For a professional finish – place the open bag over the edge of the ironing board and press thoroughly, leaving the bag to cool before moving on to the next section. Pay particular attention to the side seams and bag top.

Technique: Pressing for a Professional Finish   **>**

... and you're done.

Patchwork Cushion Cover with Zip Closure

In this project you learn how to make a simple patchwork cushion cover with zipped closure that can be made in a variety of fabrics to suit the season or the setting.

You Will Need

- **5 Fat quarters (one of these will be used as the back)**
- **1 x 16" (41cm) square of cotton batting**
- **1 12" (30cm) nylon zip in a colour to match the back**
- **Toning polyester thread**

Hand-Dyed Fabrics
A range of hand-dyed cotton fabrics are available from www.time4me-workshops.co.uk/shop.

Machine Setup

All seam allowances are ¼" (1cm) unless stated otherwise.

A 2.5mm stitch length is used throughout except for the addition of appliqué images.

A standard zig-zag foot is used throughout.

Fabric Cutting

For accuracy, all cutting should be done using a quilter's ruler and/or square and rotary cutter, unless stated otherwise.

To Make Your Cushion

Cut Out Your Pattern Pieces

1 Decide which of your 5 fat quarters you are going to use as the backing and which for the binding.

Technique: Accurate Measuring   >

2 Now cut 2 x 4 ½" (11.5cm) squares from the binding fabric and 14 x 4 ½" squares from the remaining fat quarters, so you have 16 x 4 ½" squares in total.

Technique: Rotary Cutting   >

3 Cut 2 x 16" (41cm) x 8 ½" (21.5cm) rectangles from the backing fabric.

4 Cut 4 x 3" (8cm) strips from the binding fabric.

Make Your Patchwork Panel

5 Take your 16 x 4 ½" squares and arrange them into a pleasing design.

6 Take the first two squares from the first (top) row and place them right sides together.

7 Stitch the squares together down one side using a ¼" (6mm) seam. It is not necessary to do any reverse stitching at the beginning and end of the seam as these seam ends will be stitched over when the rows are joined together.

> **Note:**
> Many sewing machine manufacturers produce a special patchwork foot, the edge of which is exactly ¼" (6mm) from the needle. If, like me, you are using a standard zig-zag foot, and you think your seam allowance is a little too wide and your machine has a facility to move the needle, you can always move the needle one or two notches to the right. The most important thing is to make all the seam allowances the same size.

8 Continue adding squares until all those from the top row are joined into a strip.

9 Repeat with the remaining rows.

10 Now using a hot steam iron, press all the seam allowances in row 1 to the left, slightly stretching the strip as you press. This helps to eliminate the little 'ledges' that can form on the right side seams.

11 Allow the strip to cool on the ironing board and then turn it over and press again, stretching it slightly and ensuring the seam allowances remain pressed in the same direction. Allow to cool.

12 Repeat with the other rows, pressing the seam allowances in row 2 to the right, row 3 to the left and row 4 to the right.

Press All Row 1 Seams
In This Direction

Press All Row 2 Seams
In This Direction

13 Now place row one face up and place row two on top, face down, lining up the vertical seams. You will find that pressing the seams in opposite directions means that they can now 'interlock' together.

14 Pin all the seams together placing the pins at 90 degrees through each seam.

15 Using a ¼" seam, stitch the two rows together, ensuring that the vertical seam allowances remain flat and in the direction in which they were pressed.

> **Note:**
> Sewing over pins is not as scary as it sounds, provided you slow down as you approach each pin. If the needle should hit a pin at a slow speed, it is likely to slide off, but if it hits at a high speed, it is likely to break the needle, or pin, or both.

16 Using a hot, steam iron, carefully press the horizontal seam open, ensuring that the vertical seam allowances remain pressed in the correct directions.

17 Repeat with the remaining two rows.

18 When all the squares are joined together and the seams thoroughly pressed, turn the piece over and press again.

Quilt Your Cushion Cover

19 Take your wadding piece and lay it face up on a flat surface (the bobbly side is the right side).

20 Lay your patchwork panel face up on top of the wadding.

21 If you are using a walking foot, use quilter's safety pins and place them in the centre of your squares securing both layers together.

22 If you are not using a walking foot, place one quilter's straight pin through each seam at 90 degrees to the seam.

23 Set your sewing machine for a 3mm straight stitch.

24 Starting with the centre seam, on one edge of your panel, stitch down the seam line.

25 Repeat with the seam lines either side of the stitched one, stitching in the same direction.

26 Turn the panel by 90 degrees and stitch down the three seam lines always stitching in the same direction.

27 Trim your quilted panel to a 16" square or, if it is too small, trim it to the largest square possible.

Insert Your Zip

28 Place the two cushion back panels right sides together.

29 Lay your zip centrally down one long edge of the panels

30 Using tailor's chalk, mark, on the cushion fabric, where the zip teeth begin and end.

31 Reset your sewing machine to a 2.5mm straight stitch.

32 Using a ½" seam allowance, stitch from the edge of the fabric to this mark.

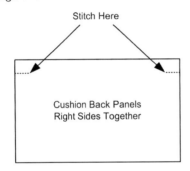

Stitch Here

Cushion Back Panels
Right Sides Together

33 Press entire seam allowance open from one seam to the other.

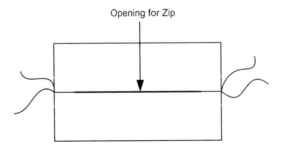

Opening for Zip

34 Turn over the joined panels and lay them on a flat surface.

35 Place the zip in the opening between the seams and pin the left-hand folded edge of the fabric close to the teeth of the zip.

36 Lap the right-hand edge slightly over the left-hand edge and pin in place, placing the pins against the teeth.

37 Tack all round the zip and remove the pins.

38 Fit a zipper foot onto your sewing machine and move the needle to the right side of the foot.

Note:
On some types of sewing machine, you may need to move the position of the foot rather than the needle.

39 Open the zip to a distance of 2". Beginning at the edge of the fabric nearest the top of the zip, stitch the left-hand side of the zip, ensuring you catch in the zip tapes, until you reach the zip pull, keeping the edge of the foot up against the teeth.

40 Stop the machine, place the needle in the fabric and raise the presser foot.

41 Close the zip, lower the presser foot and carry on stitching to the end of the fabric.

Note:
Don't be tempted to stitch around the bottom of the zip and up the other side. If you do this, it is likely that the zip will appear slightly twisted and the top edges may not lie flat.

42 Move the needle to the left side of the foot and repeat the procedure above again keeping the foot up against the teeth.

43 Lay your back panel, complete with zip, face up on a flat surface and place your quilted panel on top, face up.

44 Secure the two layers together with a few straight pins. This is to prevent the layers shifting while the binding is being added.

Add Your Binding

45 Take your four binding strips, fold them in half lengthways, and press.

46 Lay one of the binding strips onto one of the patchwork panel edges, raw edges together. Pin, placing the pins at 90 degrees to the panel edge.

47 Repeat on the opposite patchwork panel edge.

48 Trim the ends of the binding strips flush with the edges of the panel.

49 Stitch through all the layers, ¼" from the raw edges.

50 Flip the binding over to the back of the quilt and press.

51 Now fold the binding over until the folded edge meets the line of stitching. Press and pin in place, placing the pins in line with the binding.

52 Apply the remaining binding strips to the two remaining edges, leaving 1" overhang at each end. Stitch in place.

53 Turn the 1" overhang, at each end, inwards and then fold binding as before, to form a perfect corner. Pin and stitch in place using small, neat slip stitches.

54 Insert your cushion pad

... and you're done

Lined Shopping Bag

This bag has a few more features such as pockets, front and back, a separate, contrasting base with boxed corners and stronger handles stitched to the outside of the bag. The lining is inserted after the main bag body is complete.

You Will Need

- **2 x main fabric 18" x 13" (46cm x 33cm)**
- **2 x pocket fabric 18" x 9" (46cm x 23cm)**
- **1 x base fabric 18" x 9" (46cm x 23cm)**
- **2 x lining fabric 18" x 15" (46cm x 38cm)**
- **1" wide cotton webbing:
  2 yds (182cm) for short handles or 3 yds (273cm) for shoulder straps**
- **All-purpose polyester thread**

A strong cotton fabric is recommended for this bag to support all your shopping!

Hand-Dyed Fabrics
A range of hand-dyed cotton fabrics are available from www.time4me-workshops.co.uk/shop.

Machine Setup

All seam allowances are ¼" (1cm) unless stated otherwise.

A 2.5mm stitch length is used throughout except for the addition of appliqué images.

A standard zig-zag foot is used throughout.

To Make Your Bag

Cut Your Fabric Pieces

1   Measure out your fabric pieces.

Technique: Accurate Measuring	**>**

2   Using either a rotary cutter or scissors, cut out your main, pocket, base and lining fabric pieces.

Technique: Rotary Cutting	**>**

Hem Your Pockets

3   On each pocket piece, turn over one of the long edges to the wrong side by ¼"

Technique: Finishing Edges	**>**

4   Press.

Technique: Pressing for a Professional Finish	**>**

5   Turn over another 2" and press. Pin in place.

Note
Placing the pins at right angles rather than in-line with the hem means you can leave them in place while sewing.

6   Stitch close to the fold line of the ¼" turn using a standard foot, straight stitch, medium length (2.5 mm) on your sewing machine.

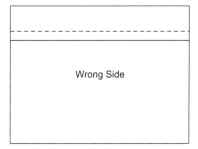

Wrong Side

Add Appliqué Designs

Note:
Before you decide on an appliqué design, it is a good idea to check where the handles of your bag are going to be, then you can ensure that your design will not be obscured by the handles.

7   If you want to add some decoration to your bag pockets such as an appliqué design, then you should do this now.

Technique: Creating Appliqué Designs   >

8   Place each pocket, right side up on the right side of each main section, lining up the lower raw edges.

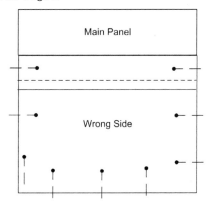

Main Panel

Wrong Side

9   Pin in place around the raw edges.

Note
Placing the pins at right angles rather than in-line with the hem means you can leave them in place while sewing.

Part-Stitch the Side Seams

10   Place the two main sections (with pockets attached) right sides together and stitch down each side seam (using a ½" seam) beginning at the top edge and stopping 6" from the bottom.

Note:
Sewing over pins is easy provided you keep your speed down. If you hit a pin at speed it is likely that the pin, and maybe the needle, will bend or break. But if you stitch slowly and hit a pin, the needle is likely to simply slide off the pin and you can carry on!

11   Press the seams open.

Turn Over the Top Hem

12   Using a 1.5mm long and 4mm wide zig-zag stitch, zig-zag around the raw edge of the bag top to prevent fraying.

13   Turn over a 2" hem around the bag top and press.

14   Pin and stitch in place using a straight stitch and toning thread.

Add the Handles

15   To mark the placement for the handles, fold the bag in vertical thirds and mark the creases.

16   Measure out your webbing depending on whether you want long or short handles.

17   Cut the webbing in two and position a length on each main section over the creases, aligning the ends with the lower raw edge.

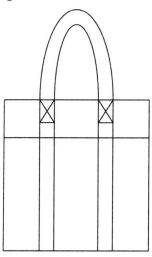

18   Stitch close to each edge of the webbing. To reinforce the handles at the top, stitch an X surrounded by a square in the hem area.

Add the Base

19 Turn the bag inside out and lay it flat on the table.

20 Turn the bottom unstitched edge back to reveal the right side of the other bottom edge.

21 Now, take the bag base piece and lay it on the bag, right side down, lining up one of the long edges with the bag bottom edge. Pin.

22 Stitch using a 2.5mm stitch length and leaving a ½" seam allowance.

23 Stitch the other long edge of the base piece to the other bag bottom edge (which was turned back).

24 Zig-zag the seam allowances together and press towards the bag bottom. Using a toning thread and a 3mm straight stitch, make a line of top-stitching ¼" from the seam on the right side.

25 Turn bag inside out and finish sewing the side seams, matching the seams where the base joins the bag bottom edges.

Box the Corners

26 To box the lower corners, fold and crease the bottom between the side seams. With the bag wrong side out, arrange each lower corner to form a point as shown, the side seam aligned with the pressed crease.

Side Seam

Bag Base

27 Stitch across approximately 1 ½" above the point keeping the stitching line perpendicular to the seam. Stitch again to reinforce.

Add the Lining

28 Place and pin the two lining sections right sides together and starting at the top of one of the short edges, and using a 2.5mm straight stitch, sew around three sides leaving a ½" seam allowance.

29 Box the corners of the lining as described for the main bag.

30 Place the lining into the bag, pushing down into the corners, and turn over the top, of the lining, to the wrong side, so the upper edge of the lining is about 1" below the top of the bag.

31 Pin the lining securely to the bag ensuring it is the same distance from the top all the way round. Hand stitch the lining securely in place using a neat slip stitch.

Technique: Basic Hand Sewing   >

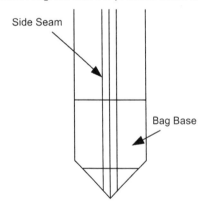

... and you're done.

Oven Gloves

Make these cheerful oven gloves, with eye-catching heart motif, or one of your own designs, in a colour scheme to match your kitchen decor. In this project you will learn about wadding and interfacing and how to enhance any sewing project by the addition of your own appliqué designs.

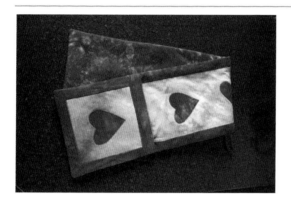

Too Hot to Handle?

I recommend you use pure cotton fabrics and wadding for this project. Pure cotton is a poor conductor of heat and provides much better insulation than other types of fabric/wadding. Polyester wadding is a good conductor of heat and using it in oven gloves will probably result in a lot of dropped dishes.

You Will Need

- **2 x fat quarters in main colour**
- **2 x fat quarters in a contrast colour (bear in mind that this fabric will be used for the heart motifs)**
- **2 x 35" x 8½" (89cm x 43cm) pieces of pure cotton batting (wadding)**
- **2 x 8½" (21cm) squares of medium-weight iron-on interfacing**
- **¼ yd (25cm) fusible web**
- **Small piece of contrast fabric for hanging loop**
- **All-purpose polyester thread in a toning colour**

A strong cotton fabric is recommended for these oven gloves.

Hand-Dyed Fabrics
A range of hand-dyed cotton fabrics are available from www.time4me-workshops.co.uk/shop.

Machine Setup

All seam allowances are ¼" (1cm) unless stated otherwise.

A 2.5mm stitch length is used throughout except for the addition of appliqué images.

A standard zig-zag foot is used throughout.

To Make Your Oven Glove

Cut out Your Oven Glove Pieces

Technique: Accurate Measuring   >

1   From the main colour, measure and cut out:
- 1 x rectangle 19" x 6" (48cm x 15cm)
- 2 x squares 6" (15cm)
- 2 x squares 8¼ " (21cm)

Technique: Rotary Cutting   >

2   From the contrast colour, measure and cut out:
- 2 x strips 1¾" x 19" (4.5cm x 48cm)
- 4 x strips 6" x 1¾" (15cm x 4.5cm)
- 4 x strips 8¼" x 1¾" (21cm x 4.5cm)
- 2 x squares 8¼" (21cm)
- 2 x rectangles 19" x 8¼" (48cm x 21cm)
- 1 x rectangle for the hanging loop 7" x 1½" (17.5cm x 4cm)

Assemble Oven Glove Main Panel

3   With right sides together, stitch the 19" x 1 ¾" contrast strips to the long edges of the 19" x 6" rectangle.

4 Press the seam allowances open.

> **Technique:** Pressing for a Professional Finish >

5 Place the 8 ¼" main colour squares, one on each end of the rectangle, wrong sides together. Line up one of the sides of each square with the short ends of the rectangle. Pin these ends together.

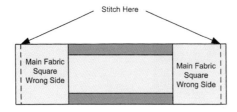

6 Stitch the 8¼" main colour squares to the short ends of the rectangle.

7 Open out the squares and press seam allowances towards the squares.

Make the Hand Pockets

8 Take one of the 6" main colour squares and stitch two of the 6" contrast strips to opposite sides. Press seam allowances open.

9 Stitch two of the 8¼" strips to the remaining sides. Press seam allowances open.

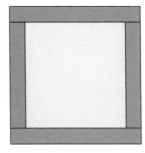

10 Repeat with the remaining 6" main colour square.

11 Using a dry iron, set to the 'wool' setting, fuse a 8¼" square of interfacing to the rear of each of these blocks.

> **Tip:** Choosing and Using Interfacing >

12 Now place one of the 8¼" contrast squares right sides together on top of each of these blocks and stitch down one edge creating a ¼" seam.

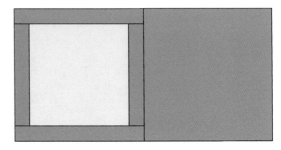

13 Open out blocks and press seam towards the edged block. Fold the plain square over onto the rear of the edged square and press with wrong sides together to form a faced block.

Add Your Heart Appliqués

14 If you want to add an appliqué design, then you can do this now.

> **Technique:** Creating Appliqué Designs >

15 Trace the heart image, below, onto the fusible web five times, keeping the images close together.

16 Roughly cut out the block of hearts. If you are using fusible web which has two paper backings, remove one paper backing ensuring that the glue layer remains with the side on which you have traced your image.

17 Position the block of hearts onto the wrong side of a piece of the contrast fabric. When you are happy with the positioning, press in place using a dry iron set to the wool setting. Allow to cool.

Note:
If you only have one iron and don't want to risk getting glue on the soleplate, you can increase the iron temperature a little and use a pressing cloth when fusing your appliqué images.

18 Carefully cut out each heart.

19 Remove the paper backing from two of the hearts, and place in the centre of each of the hand pocket blocks, orientating the hearts as required. In the following diagram, the seam joining the facing and the block is at the bottom.

20 Fuse in place.

21 Set your sewing machine for a narrow zig-zag or blanket stitch and stitch around the heart shapes, through the pocket top and facing.

22 Fuse and stitch the remaining three hearts to the main section of the glove as shown.

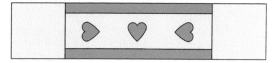

Assemble Your Oven Glove

23 Lay the main section of the glove on a flat surface, right side up.

24 Place the hand pockets on each end, right side up with the seam facing towards the centre of the glove and the raw outer edges aligned.

25 Stitch together the two 19" x 8¼" rectangles along one of their short edges. Press seam open.

26 Place this piece on top of the glove panel followed by the two pieces of batting.

Tip: Selecting and Using Wadding   >

27 Trim all the layers to the same size.

28 Ensuring that the hand pockets remain in position, pin layers together all the way round leaving a 6" gap along one of the long edges for turning.

29 Stitch, ½" in from the edge beginning at one side of the gap and finishing at the other side.

31

30 Using scissors, trim the batting close to the seams.

31 Turn right side out and press.

Make a Hanging Loop

32 Take the fabric cut for the hanging loop and iron over ¼" on one long edge.

33 Turn in the other long edge to the centre of the fabric and iron.

34 Fold the first edge into the centre covering the raw edge.

35 Pin and stitch one line of stitching along the length of the piece.

> **Note**
> Placing the pins at right angles rather than in-line with the edge means you can leave them in place while sewing.

36 Position the hanging loop in the centre of the glove and stitch to the seam allowance of the gap left open for turning.

37 Close the gap with neat hand-stitching.

> **Technique:** Basic Hand Sewing   >

... and you're done.

Tea Cosy

Make this cheerful tea cosy to match your oven gloves, or make one as a gift for a special friend. In this project you will learn how to quilt your design and create neat bound edges.

Too Hot to Handle?

I recommend you use pure cotton fabrics and wadding for this project. Pure cotton is a poor conductor of heat and provides much better insulation than other types of fabric/wadding. Polyester wadding is a good conductor of heat and will probably result in your tea getting cold more quickly.

You Will Need

- **3 x contrasting fat quarters of pure cotton fabric**
- **½yd (½m) pure cotton wadding**
- **½yd (½m) lining fabric**
- **Fabric for 3 x heart appliqué shapes**
- **Fusible web for heart appliqué shapes**
- **Fabric for hanging loop**
- **All purpose polyester thread in a toning colour**

Hand-Dyed Fabrics
A range of hand-dyed cotton fabrics are available from www.time4me-workshops.co.uk/shop.

Machine Setup

All seam allowances are ¼" (1cm) unless stated otherwise.

A 2.5mm stitch length is used throughout except for the addition of appliqué images.

A standard zig-zag foot is used throughout.

To Make Your Cosy

Cut Your Pattern Pieces

1 From each of the fat quarters, cut 2 x rectangles 4½" x 10½" (12cm x 27cm).

Technique: Rotary Cutting   >

2 From the remainder of one of the fat quarters cut two strips 4" (10cm) x 15" (38cm). These will be joined together to form the gusset.

3 From the remainder of one of the other fat quarters cut sufficient 3" wide binding to fit around the bottom of the tea cosy plus 4" to allow for seam allowances and joining.

Technique: Binding Edges   >

4 From the same fabric, cut a strip 6" (15cm) x 2" (5cm) for the hanging loop.

5 From the wadding, cut two rectangles 12" (30cm) x 10½" (27cm) (for the front and back) and one long gusset strip 4" (10cm) x 29" (74cm).

Tip: Selecting and Using Wadding   >

6 From the lining fabric, cut two rectangles 12" (30cm) x 10½" (27cm) (for the front and back) and one long gusset strip 4" (10cm) x 29" (74cm).

Assemble Your Front and Back Panels and Gusset Section

7 Leaving a ¼" seam, stitch together three patchwork panels, by their long edges, for the front and back of the cosy.

Technique: Finishing Edges   >

8 Press seams open.

> **Technique:** Pressing for a Professional Finish **>**

9 Lay each panel right side down and lay a wadding panel on top followed by a lining panel.

10 Using a walking foot, if you have one, quilt the panels in a crosshatch design, shown below.

> **Technique:** Basic Machine Quilting **>**

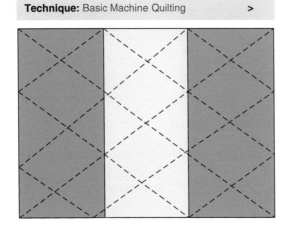

Make Your Appliqué Hearts

11 If you want to add the heart appliqué design, then you can do this now.

> **Technique:** Creating Appliqué Designs **>**

12 Trace 3 x appliqué heart shapes, shown below, onto the fusible web – keep them close together.

13 Roughly cut around the group of heart shapes and iron onto the back of the fabric you have chosen for the appliqué.

14 Cut out the individual heart shapes.

15 Remove the paper backing from the hearts and press onto the front panel as shown in the picture.

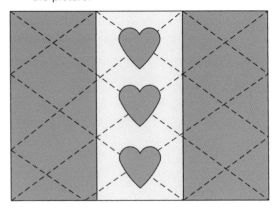

16 Set a dry iron to a medium setting and press the hearts in position.

17 Set the sewing machine for a medium zig-zag or blanket stitch and sew round each heart.

Assemble Your Tea Cosy

18 Fold each of the quilted panels in half widthways.

19 To make a paper pattern for your cosy as shown in the diagram below, take a sheet of A4 paper and draw a curve as shown in the diagram.

> **Note:**
> If you are not confident with drawing the curve freehand you can use a flexible dressmakers curve. The curve does not have to be exactly as shown as long as you end up with an approximate T-cosy shape! Do however make sure that the fold of your quilted panel is on the side of your pattern that WILL NOT be cut, as, if it is, the resulting panel will not fit any sort of teapot.

20 Lay the paper pattern onto to each of the quilted panels, ensuring that the folded edge is on the side of the pattern that will not be cut, and cut to shape.

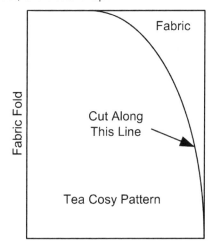

21 Stitch the two strips of gusset fabric together along the short ends to form a strip 4" x 29" (10cm x 74cm). Press the seam open.

22 Make a quilting sandwich by laying the gusset lining piece on a flat surface wrong side up, followed by the gusset wadding, followed by the gusset fabric right side up. Pin and quilt as before or just by using straight lines of stitching, as in the photograph.

Make a Hanging Loop

23 Find the top centre point of each of the front and back panels and mark with tailors chalk. (This is where the hanging loop will be inserted).

24 With the right sides together, pin the front and back quilted panels to either side of the gusset marking the point where the hanging loop will go.

25 Press the fabric for the hanging loop then fold one long edge into the centre of the piece and press again.

26 Fold the other long edge in by ¼", or to meet the raw edge from the first fold, and press. Then fold over again to overlap the first edge.

27 Press and stitch down the centre of the piece to secure the edges.

28 Place the loop inside the cosy and insert the ends through the gusset seam at the marked points.

29 Allow the ends to protrude about ½" above the seam allowance and pin securely in place. Ensure that the loop is not twisted.

30 Stitch all round the gusset seams using a ½" seam allowance.

> **Note:**
> If you have used a fabric that is prone to fraying you could zig-zag round the gusset seam allowances or even bind them in a toning colour. See Add Binding to the Lower Edge.

Add Binding to the Lower Edge

31 Using a ¼" seam, join all the binding strips together by their short sides and press the seams open.

32 Now lay the strip on your ironing board and fold in half along its length. Press.

33 Starting at the lower centre back of the cosy, pin the binding around the lower edge, lining up the raw edges of the binding with those of the cosy.

34 When you have pinned all the way round, trim the overlap to 1" and then turn over ½" to the wrong side of the strip and press.

35 Place this turned in end over the raw end that you started with and pin in place.

36 Stitch the binding to the tea cosy ¼" from the raw edge.

37 Now flip the binding over so the folded edge meets the row of stitching on the inside of the cosy. Press.

38 Slip stitch neatly in place.

Technique: Basic Hand Sewing	>

... and you're done.

Tablecloth

This fun tablecloth will draw admiring comments at your summer barbecue but the border and colours could also be customised for other seasons such as using leaves for autumn and Christmas images for the festive season. In this project you will learn how to create one of the most common patchwork design patterns, called "flying geese" and learn how to do free-machine embroidery.

You Will Need

- **3 toning fat quarters in each of four colours. I have used three different values (light, medium and dark) in violet, cherry, green and orange.**
- **1m fabric for wide borders**
- **1½ m fabric for backing. If your fabric is only 45" wide you will need to join it to make the 47" width.**
- **½ m fabric for binding**
- **Fabric scraps for appliqué images**
- **1m Steam-a-Seam for appliqué images**
- **Template for appliqué images.**

Hand-Dyed Fabrics
A range of hand-dyed cotton fabrics are available from www.time4me-workshops.co.uk/shop.

Machine Setup

All seam allowances are ¼" (1cm) unless stated otherwise.

A 2.5mm stitch length is used throughout except for the addition of appliqué images.

A standard zig-zag foot is used throughout except for the addition of appliqué images.

To Make Your Tablecloth

Cut Out Your Fabric

1　Cut out the following pieces:

- 5 x squares 5¼" (13cm) in the light or medium value of each of the four colours
- 20 x squares $2^7/_8$" (7.5cm) in the light or medium value of each of the four colours
- 10 x squares 2½" x 8½" (6½cm x 21½ cm) in the dark value of each of the four colours
- 4 x strips 32" x 8½" (81½"cm x 21½"cm) for wide borders
- 1 x backing piece 47" x 47" (120cm x 120cm)

Technique: Rotary Cutting　　　　　　　　　>

Make Your Flying Geese Squares

2　Lay one 5¼" square face up on a flat surface.

3　Place two $2^7/_8$" squares (in the same colour range) face down on the larger square.

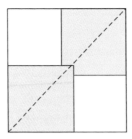

4 Draw a diagonal line through both small squares as shown.

5 Check that your needle is in the centre position and line up one edge of your presser foot with the diagonal line. Stitch. Repeat on the other side of the line.

Technique: Finishing Edges   >

6 Using a rotary cutter and ruler, cut along the diagonal line.

7 Press the small triangles away from the large ones, pressing the seam allowance towards the large triangle.

Technique: Pressing for a Professional Finish   >

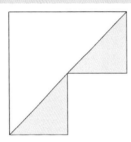

8 Place one small square face down on each of the two triangle pieces and draw a diagonal line as shown.

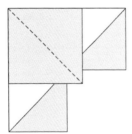

9 Stitch, as before, on either side of the diagonal line.

10 Cut along the diagonal line.

11 Press the small triangles away from the large one, pressing the seam allowances towards the large triangle. This makes one flying

geese panel. Make a further three in the same way.

12 Join the four panels to form a block as shown below.

13 Lay one of the 2½" x 8½" strips (in the same colour range), wrong side up along one of the long edges of the block. Pin in place. Repeat with another strip on the other long edge of the block.

14 Stitch the strips onto the blocks. Press seams towards long strips.

15 Make all 20 blocks in the same manner.

16 Press thoroughly.

17 Using a quilter's square and rotary cutter, trim all blocks to 8 ¼" square.

Assemble Your Tablecloth Centre

18 Arrange 16 of the blocks into a pleasing arrangement. An example is shown below. See the photograph for some colour arrangement ideas.

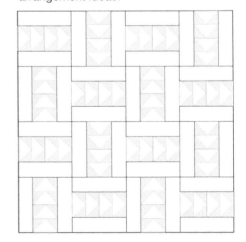

19 Lay the first block face down onto the second and pin the edge to be stitched. Stitch. Join the remaining blocks in the row. Seam allowances will naturally lie in the direction they need to be pressed.

20 Complete remaining rows in a similar manner.

21 Lay row one face down onto row 2 and pin in place, lining up seams accurately. Stitch, making sure that all seam allowances stay lying in the direction they were pressed.

22 Repeat with remaining rows.

23 Give the whole piece a good steam press, ensuring seam allowances stay in position.

Make Your Borders

24 Trace the appliqué shapes onto fusible web. Group similar items together as closely as possible. To create the design show at the beginning of this project, you will need:

- 4 x orange outlines
- 32 x orange segments
- 4 x apple outlines
- 4 x apple cores
- 4 x bunches of grapes
- 4 x grape stalks
- 24 x cherries (or more, if you particularly like cherries)

25 Using scissors, roughly cut out each group of shapes keeping those of the same colour together.

26 Remove one paper backing from the pieces ensuring that the glue layer remains with the remaining paper backing (the one you traced the shapes onto).

27 Finger press each group of shapes onto the appropriate colour fabric.

28 Press with a medium dry iron.

29 Carefully cut out the shapes and divide them into four groups with sufficient pieces, for each border, in each group.

30 Press one of the border pieces and lay it flat on the table.

31 Arrange the appliqué shapes until you are happy with the design. An example is shown below for the main fruits. Add as many cherries as you like!

32 Once you are satisfied with the design, remove the paper backings and press the pieces into place using a medium iron.

33 Set your machine for free-machine embroidery and, using appropriately coloured machine-embroidery threads, stitch pieces in place. Add lines for the orange segments and circles for grapes.

Technique: Free-machine Embroidery   **>**

Note

If you have not had a lot of experience in free-machine embroidery, you may prefer to secure your appliqué shapes with a narrow zig-zag or blanket stitch.

34 Add embroidered (or satin-stitch) cherry stalks.

35 Repeat for remaining border pieces

Assemble Your Tablecloth

36 Lay one of the border pieces face down along one edge of your flying geese panel, lining up the raw edges. Pin in place. Repeat with another border piece on the opposite edge. Stitch in place.

37 Open out the borders and press the seam allowances toward the borders.

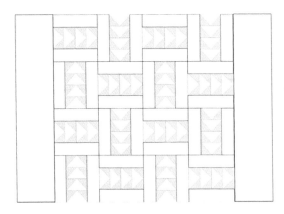

38 Take one of the remaining 8½" border pieces and attach one flying geese block to each end, ensuring that the seams line up with the joining seam lines of the first two borders.

39 Stitch the borders, with the flying geese panels attached, to the tablecloth as shown below.

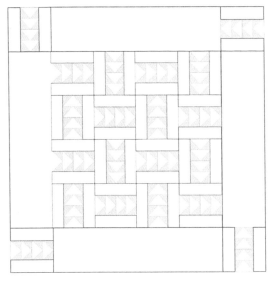

40 Press all border seam allowances towards borders.

41 Give the backing fabric a good press and lay it flat on the table.

42 Lay the tablecloth on top and carefully cut backing to the same size.

43 Securely pin together the tablecloth top and backing.

44 Using a walking foot if you have one, quilt (using a 3mm stitch) along all of the seam lines, which join the flying geese panels together, ensuring the backing remains flat.

Technique: Basic Machine Quilting   >

Add Your Binding

45 Prepare a double-thickness binding strip(s) and iron down the centre.

Technique: Binding Edges   >

46 Pin your binding to your table cloth.

47 Machine-stitch the binding in place on one side then fold the binding over the edge of the table cloth and hand-stitch the other side using a neat slip stitch.

48 Remove pins from the binding.

49 Give the whole tablecloth a final good, steam press and admire!

Technique: Pressing for a Professional Finish   >

... and you're done.

Table Runner

Make this simple table runner in a variety of colours to suit your mood. Then collect seasonal leaves and make appliqué shapes to decorate it. Choose the deciduous greens and yellows for summer, the bronze and red of fallen leaves for autumn, or holly and ivy for Christmas. For beginners, the runner can be left plain. In this project you will learn more about binding edges and gain confidence in using appliqué.

What is a 'Fat Quarter'?

You may see 'Fat Quarters' of fabric for sale in the shops. These are rough squares of fabric, generally for patchwork use, produced by cutting a metre (or a yard) of length of a roll of fabric.

Rolls of fabric are typically 40 to 45 inches wide, depending on the manufacturer. The resultant strip of fabric (either 1 m or 1 yrd long by 40 to 45 inches wide) is then cut into four to create four Fat Quarters.

The minimum dimensions for a Fat Quarter should therefore be 18 x 20 inches), allowing you to get nine 6 x 6 inch squares for your patchwork. The edges are often not cut straight and will need 'squaring up' with a Rotary Cutter and Ruler.

Similarly, 'Fat Eighths' are half this size (18 x 10 inches).

You Will Need

- **3 fat quarters in harmonizing shades (you won't need all this fabric but can use the leftovers to make the matching tablemats)**
- **1 fat quarter in a contrasting shade**
- **½ m x 45" contrasting fabric for binding (use the remainder for the table mat binding)**
- **¾m pure cotton batting (at least 45" or 115cm wide)**
- **¾m backing fabric (at least 45" or 115cm wide). If you choose a decorative backing fabric your table runner will be double-sided!**
- **Toning polyester thread**
- **Embroidery threads**
- **1m fusible web**
- **Collect seasonal leaves from your garden or the park to make appliqué templates. Press flat between two sheets of kitchen paper and place between the pages of a heavy book. Alternatively, use the supplied templates.**

Hand-Dyed Fabrics
A range of hand-dyed cotton fabrics are available from www.time4me-workshops.co.uk/shop.

Machine Setup

All seam allowances are ¼" (1cm) unless stated otherwise.

A 2.5mm stitch length is used throughout except for the addition of appliqué images.

A standard zig-zag foot is used throughout except for the addition of appliqué images.

Fabric Cutting

For accuracy, all cutting should be done using a quilter's ruler and rotary cutter, unless stated otherwise.

To Make Your Runner

1   From each of the three harmonizing fabrics, cut 5 pieces 3½" x 11" (9cm x 28cm), giving 15 pieces in total.

Technique: Rotary Cutting   >

2 From the contrasting fat quarter, cut 15 x 3½" squares.

3 From the binding fabric, cut three strips 45" x 3" (115cm x 8cm).

4 From the batting, cut a piece 46" x 15" (117cm x 38cm)

5 From the backing fabric, cut a piece 46" x 15" (117cm x 38cm)

Make Your Runner Top

6 Place one of the contrasting squares, right sides together against one of the short edges of one of the rectangles and stitch in place, leaving a ¼" seam.

7 Repeat for the remaining rectangles and squares.

8 Press the seam allowances towards the rectangles.

Technique: Pressing for a Professional Finish   >

9 Arrange your blocks as shown in the diagram, moving the colours around until you are happy with the result.

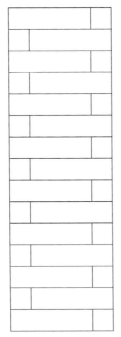

10 Starting at the top, place one of the blocks on top of the one immediately below, right sides together and stitch along one of the long edges.

11 Repeat until all the blocks are joined together.

12 Press all the seam allowances open

Quilt Your Runner

13 Place your backing fabric face down on a flat surface and lay the batting on top.

14 Lay the pieced and pressed runner on top, right side up.

15 Using long quilting pins (the flower-headed ones are good as they don't catch in the machine foot), place two pins along each of the long seams, at 90 degrees to the seam, through all three layers. Place the pins about 5" apart. Fit a walking foot to your machine if you have one.

16 Increase the machine stitch length to 3mm.

17 Using a harmonizing thread on the top and a thread that matches the backing on the bobbin, quilt down each of the long seams, beginning near the centre of the runner and working towards the ends.

Technique: Basic Machine Quilting   >

18 Trim the runner so it measures 44" x 14" (112cm x 36cm).

Make Your Appliqué Leaves

19 If you want to add the appliqué leaves, then you can do this now. For alternative design ideas, see the following skill sheet.

Technique: Creating Appliqué Designs   >

20 Trace the outlines of the leaves onto the fusible web and roughly cut out each leaf.

21 Press each leaf shape on to the back of the chosen fabric using a dry iron set to the wool setting.

22 Cut out leaf shapes carefully.

23 Remove the paper backing and position your leaves across the runner top.

24 When you are happy with their position press in place.

25 Using free-machine embroidery, secure
each leaf in place adding veins and stalks as
required.

Technique: Free-machine Embroidery   >

Note
If you don't feel confident enough to use free-
machine embroidery, secure the leaves using a zig-
zag or blanket stitch.

Add Your Binding

26 Prepare a double-thickness binding strip(s)
and iron down the centre.

Technique: Binding Edges   >

27 Pin your binding to your runner.

28 Machine-stitch the binding in place on one
side then fold the binding over the edge of
the table cloth and hand-stitch the other side
using a neat slip stitch.

29 Remove pins from the binding.

30 Give the table runner a final good, steam
press and admire!

Technique: Pressing for a Professional Finish   >

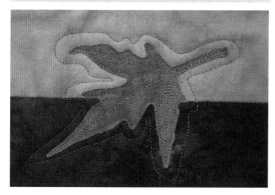

... and you're done.

Table Mats

Make these simple table mats, to match your new runner, in a variety of colours to suit your mood. Then collect seasonal leaves and make appliqué shapes to decorate. Choose florals in hues of greens and yellows for summer, colours of fallen leaves for autumn, or something warm and spicy for Christmas. In this project you will learn about binding edges and creating your own appliqué templates from leaves.

This project makes four table mats of finished size 11" (28cm) x 12" (30cm).

You Will Need

- **1 fat quarter, similar to the harmonizing shades used in the runner, for the table mat centres**
- **4 fat quarters in harmonizing shades (use the leftover pieces from the runner for three of the colours)**
- **1 fat quarter in a contrasting shade**
- **½ m x 45" contrasting fabric for binding (or use the remaining binding fabric from the runner)**
- **½ m pure cotton batting (at least 45" or 115cm wide) or use the remaining batting from the runner.**
- **½ m backing fabric (at least 45" or 115cm wide) or use the remaining backing from the runner (If you choose a decorative backing fabric your table mats will be double-sided!)**
- **¼ m Steam-a-seam fusible web**
- **Fabric scraps for appliqué leaves**

- **Seasonal leaves to make appliqué templates – pressed flat between two sheets of kitchen paper and placed between the pages of a heavy book. Or use supplied templates.**
- **Toning polyester thread**

Hand-Dyed Fabrics
A range of hand-dyed cotton fabrics are available from www.time4me-workshops.co.uk/shop.

Machine Setup

All seam allowances are ¼" (1cm) unless stated otherwise.

A 2.5mm stitch length is used throughout except for the addition of appliqué images.

A standard zig-zag foot is used throughout except for the addition of appliqué images.

Fabric Cutting

For accuracy, all cutting should be done using a quilter's ruler and rotary cutter, unless stated otherwise.

To Make Four Table Mats

Cut Out Your Patchwork Pieces

1   For the table mat centre fabric, cut 4 x rectangles 5½" (14cm) x 6½" (15cm).

Technique: Rotary Cutting   >

2   From each of two of the harmonizing fabrics, cut 4 pieces 3½" (9cm) x 5½" (14cm), giving 8 pieces in total.

3   From the other two harmonizing fabrics, cut 4 pieces 3½" (9cm) x 6½" (17cm), giving 8 pieces in total.

4   From the contrasting fat quarter, cut 16 x 3½" squares.

5   From the binding fabric, cut 3 x strips 45" x 3" (115cm x 8cm).

6   From the batting, cut 4 x pieces 12" x 13" (30cm x 32.5cm)

7   From the backing fabric, cut 4 x pieces 12" x 13" (30cm x 32.5cm)

Make Your Mat Tops

8   Place one of the contrasting squares, right sides together against one of the short edges of one of the 5½"rectangles and stitch along the short edge. Repeat for the other end of the same rectangle.

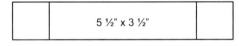
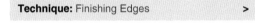

5 ½" x 3 ½"

Technique: Finishing Edges   **>**

9   Repeat for the remaining 5½" x 3½" rectangles You should now have 8 blocks of 11½" x 3½ " (28cm x 9cm) and 8 blocks of 6½" x 3½" (17cm x 9cm).

10   Press the seam allowances towards the rectangles.

Technique: Pressing for a Professional Finish   **>**

11   Arrange your blocks as shown in the diagram, ensuring you have one of each of the four harmonizing colours in each mat and moving the colours around until you are happy with the result.

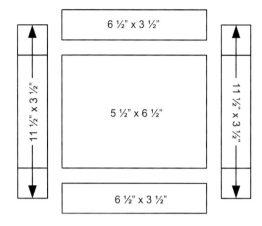

6 ½" x 3 ½"

11 ½" x 3 ½"

5 ½" x 6 ½"

11 ½" x 3 ½"

6 ½" x 3 ½"

12   Stitch the 6 ½" x 3 ½" blocks to the longest sides of the mat centre leaving a ¼" seam.

13   Press seam allowance towards block.

14   Stitch the longer blocks to the mat centre as shown being careful to line up the seams.

Quilt Your Mats

15   Place one piece of backing fabric face down on a flat surface and lay one piece cotton batting on top.

Tip: Selecting and Using Wadding   **>**

16   Lay the pieced and pressed mat on top, right side up.

17   Using long quilting pins (the flower-headed ones are good as they don't catch in the machine foot), place two pins along each of the long seams, at 90 degrees to the seam, through all three layers. Place the pins about 5" apart.

18   Fit a walking foot to your machine if you have one and increase the machine stitch length to 3mm.

19   Using a harmonizing thread on the top and a thread that matches the backing on the bobbin.

20   Line up the centre mark on the walking foot with the top end of one of the long seams and stitch along the length of the seam doing a few reverse stitches at the beginning and end of the seam. As you stitch, ease the fabric, at either side of the seam, apart so the stitching sinks into the seam.

21 Trim off threads.

> **Technique:** Basic Machine Quilting   >

22 Trim each mat so it measures 11" (28cm) x 12" (30cm).

Make Your Appliqué Leaves

23 If you want to add the appliqué leaves, then you can do this now.

> **Technique:** Creating Appliqué Designs   >

24 Trace the outlines of four large leaves (or more if you want) onto the fusible web and roughly cut out each leaf.

25 Press each leaf shape on to the back of the chosen fabric using a dry iron set to the wool setting.

26 Cut out leaf shapes carefully.

27 Remove the paper backing and position your leaves on the mat tops.

28 When you are happy with their position, press in place.

29 Using free-machine embroidery, secure each leaf in place adding veins and stalks as required.

> **Technique:** Free-machine Embroidery   >

> **Note**
> If you don't feel confident enough to use free-machine embroidery, secure the leaves using a narrow zig-zag or blanket stitch.

Add Your Binding

30 Prepare a double-thickness binding strip(s) and iron down the centre.

> **Technique:** Binding Edges   >

31 Pin your binding to your mat.

32 Machine-stitch the binding in place on one side then fold the binding over the edge of the table cloth and hand-stitch the other side using a neat slip stitch.

33 Remove pins, give the table mat a final good, steam press and admire!

> **Technique:** Pressing for a Professional Finish   >

... and you're done.

Hot Water Bottle Cover

Make this as a gift for someone special or just treat yourself. The large top flap on the top of this cover allows for easy filling of the bottle and a hanging loop allows for easy storage. The images given are just a suggestion, any winter or sleep related motif would be suitable. In this project you will learn how to make a split back (to insert the hot water bottle) and gain more practice in quilting.

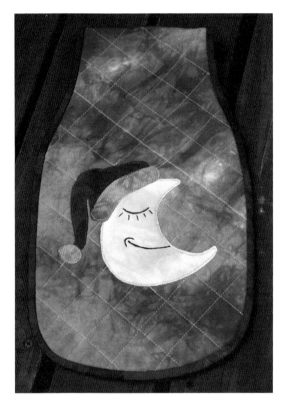

This project makes a single hot water bottle cover for any size of hot water bottle.

You Will Need

- ½ m of sturdy cotton fabric
- 1 x fat quarter of contrast cotton fabric for piping
- ½ m of pure cotton batting
- ½ m thin cotton for lining
- ½ m fusible web
- Scraps of fabric for appliqué
- 1" square of Velcro for flap
- Toning threads
- Hot Water Bottle

Hand-Dyed Fabrics
A range of hand-dyed cotton fabrics are available from www.time4me-workshops.co.uk/shop.

Machine Setup

All seam allowances are ¼" (1cm) unless stated otherwise.

A 2.5mm stitch length is used throughout except for the addition of appliqué images.

A standard zig-zag foot is used throughout.

Fabric Cutting

For accuracy, all cutting should be done using a quilter's ruler and/or square and rotary cutter, unless stated otherwise. The exception to this is when cutting out appliqué images when scissors can be used.

To Make Your Hot Water Bottle Cover

Cut Out Your Pattern

1   Lay a large sheet of paper (any sort will do) out on a flat surface and place your (empty) hot water bottle on it.

2   Draw round the bottle adding ½" seam allowance all the way round.

3   Cut one back piece the size of the template.

4   Using the template as a pattern, cut out one front piece, extending the top so it is long enough to fold over the top of the bottle and fasten on the other side.

5 Using the front and back pieces as patterns, cut out one of each of batting and lining.

| **Tip:** Selecting and Using Wadding | > |

Add Your Appliqué

6 If you want to add an appliqué design, then you can do this now.

| **Technique:** Creating Appliqué Designs | > |

7 Trace the appliqué image onto fusible web.

8 Roughly cut around each shape and, using a dry iron set to the wool setting, press onto the back of the fabric you are using for the appliqué.

9 Carefully cut out the images from the fabric.

10 Arrange the images on the front outer panel of the cover and, once you are happy with the arrangement, press in place.

11 Set your sewing machine for a 3mm wide, 2mm length zig-zag stitch and, using a toning thread carefully stitch around the images.

Note:
If you prefer to use blanket stitch instead of zig-zag, this would be equally effective. If you do decided to use free-machine embroidery, place the lining and batting panel behind the front outer panel before you stitch the image pieces in place, stitching through all three layers.

Quilt Your Cover

| **Technique:** Basic Machine Quilting | > |

12 Take the lining panel for the front cover and lay out on a flat surface. Lay the front batting panel on top followed by the front cotton panel, right side up.

Note:
There are a number of ways in which this project can be quilted, depending on your personal taste. You could either quilt around the image, or if you are experienced in free-machine machine quilting, you could make an all-over star pattern. Personally, I prefer to cross-hatch quilt a project such as this.

13 Pin the three layers together securely

14 Fit a walking foot – if you have one – to your sewing machine and, using toning thread and a 3mm straight stitch, quilt the front panel, stopping at the edges of the image and continuing on the other side so the image remains unquilted. Ensure that you do a few reverse stitches when stopping and starting at the edges of the image, or the stitches may begin to unravel.

Note:
You are probably wondering if it wouldn't be easier to quilt the front panel before adding the image. I have tried this but find that the quilted lines show through the image when it is fused to the panel and detract from the effect.

15 Layer and quilt the back section with the cross-hatch design.

Divide and Bind the Back Section

16 Take the back section and measure and mark a point 6" from the bottom of the panel. Cut the panel in half, widthways (from side to side) through this point.

17 Measure one of the edges you have just cut and cut two pieces of fabric of this length and 3" wide.

| **Technique:** Finishing Edges | > |

18 Fold each piece in half lengthways and press.

19 Pin one piece to each of the cut edges, on the right side of the panel and with the raw edges together. Place your pins at 90 degrees to the edge so you can sew over them.

Note:
Sewing over pins is not as scary as it sounds, provided you slow down as you approach each pin. If the needle should hit a pin at a slow speed, it is likely to slide off, but if it hits at a high speed, it is likely to break the needle, or pin, or both.

20 Stitch both bindings in place.

21 Flip the binding over and press then fold toward the back of the panel, lining the folded edge up with the line of stitching.

Press and pin in place, again placing the
pins at 90 degrees.

22 Repeat for the top edge of the back top
panel.

23 Stitch binding to both edges, from the right
side of the panel, positioning your stitches
1/8" from the seam joining the binding to the
panel.

24 Place the front panel, face down on a table,
then place the back panels on top, face up,
lapping the top back binding over the lower
back binding.

25 Pin the 6 layers together at several places
around the panel.

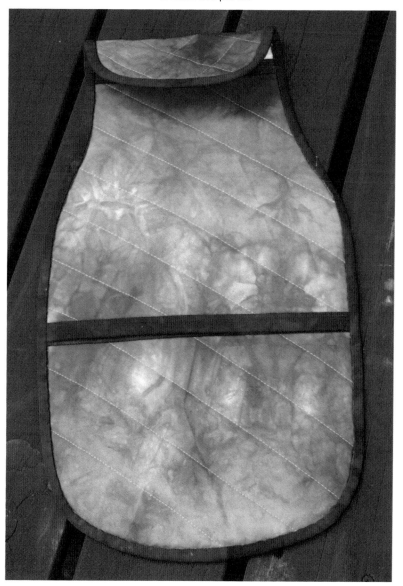

Add Your Binding

26 Make the binding.

Technique: Binding Edges   >

27 Turn the cover over so the front is facing
upwards.

28 Starting at the centre of the lower edge of the
cover and leaving a 2" end, pin the binding
all round the bottle cover front, raw edges
together, finishing with a 2" end at the point
where you started.

Note:
When pinning on the binding, ensure that you catch
in the back panel and the wadding and lining of the
extended top edge.

29 Open out the 2" ends, unpicking a few
stitches if necessary, and pin them right
sides together so they will lie flat against the
edge of the cover.

30 Stitch and trim seam allowances to ½".

31 Press seam open.

32 Fold the binding in half to cover the seam,
press and pin in place.

Make a Hanging Loop

33 Cut a piece of leftover binding fabric about
6" long.

34 Turn over one long edge ¼" and press.

35 Turn over the other long edge ½" and press.

36 Fold the first edge over the second,
enclosing the raw edges and press and pin
at 90 degrees to the strip.

37 Stitch down the centre of the strip close to the centre fold.

38 Fold strip in half and pin to the back lower edge, in the centre, raw edges together, so the loop is pointing upwards.

39 Stitch the binding all round the cover ¼" from the edge, securing the loop in place at the same time.

40 Using scissors, trim around the edge of the cover so the edges are flush with the binding edges.

41 Fold the binding over towards the back of the cover so the folded edge meets the stitching.

42 Pin, press and stitch, using a neat slip stitch, in place.

Fasten Your Cover Top

43 Stitch one side(hook or loop) of your Velcro to the cover top back, ensuring it is centralised, and one to the underside of the flap.

... and you're done

Patchwork Quilt

Make yourself a quilt in soft shades of pinks, lilacs and purples (or any other harmonious colours). Then add some contrasting appliqué hearts (or other design) for that personal touch. Recycled men's shirts can provide high quality fabrics for your quilt. In this project you will improve your cutting and quilting skills.

This project makes a quilt measuring 67" x 77" (170cm x 196cm).

Sufficient fabric for the quilt can be cut from six, large, long-sleeved, men's shirts. It is best to use good quality shirts with a soft handle as the fabric will be more stable and will last longer. See my video at *** for details of cutting up shirts into usable fabric.

You Will Need

- **44 x 10" (25cm) squares in 6 assorted colours**
- **298" of 5" (12.5cm) strips in 6 assorted colours for border**
- **88 x 4" (10cm) squares in 6 assorted colours for binding**
- **Fusible web for 4 heart shapes**
- **Heart template (provided at the end of these instructions).**
- **2m of 90" (130cm) wide pure cotton wadding such as Warm 'n' Natural.**

- **2m of 90" (130cm) wide backing fabric such as polycotton sheeting.**
- **30 buttons no larger than ½" (1cm shirt buttons) diameter.**
- **All-purpose polyester thread in a toning colour**
- **Toning quilting thread for sewing on buttons.**

Hand-Dyed Fabrics
A range of hand-dyed cotton fabrics are available from www.time4me-workshops.co.uk/shop.

Machine Setup

All seam allowances are ¼" (1cm) unless stated otherwise.

A 2.5mm stitch length is used throughout except for the addition of appliqué images.

A standard zig-zag foot is used throughout.

Fabric Cutting

For accuracy, all cutting should be done using a quilter's ruler and/or square and rotary cutter, unless stated otherwise. The exception to this is when cutting out appliqué images when scissors can be used.

To Make Your Quilt

Cut Your Quilt Pieces

1   Using a rotary cutter, cut 44 squares of 10" in assorted colours for your quilt front.

Technique: Rotary Cutting   >

2   Cut 298" of fabric in 5" strips for the quilt front. These will be positioned on the quilt front around the edge of the quilting squares.

3   Cut 84 4" squares of 4" for your binding.

4   Cut 2m of 90" wide backing fabric.

Arrange Your Squares

5   Take 42 of the 10" squares, reserving two of the same design for the heart motifs.

6   Arrange the squares into a block 6 squares x 7 squares, moving them around until you are happy with the arrangement.

> **Note:**
> To help you decide if the arrangement is suitable, stand back from the blocks and squint your eyes. If any of the blocks appear more prominent than the others, they are probably in the wrong place and need rearranging. This is also a good method for gauging whether colours go together.

Add Your Heart Motifs

7   Choose four squares to be embellished with heart motifs. Either choose dark squares and light hearts or light squares and dark hearts.

> **Technique:** Creating Appliqué Designs   >

8   Trace four heart shapes onto the paper side of the fusible web and cut out.

9   Iron the heart shapes, glue side down, onto the squares reserved in step 1.

10 Cut out hearts and iron on to the squares chosen in step 3.

11 Set your sewing machine to a narrow zig-zag (3-4mm width and 1.5mm length) or blanket

stitch and stitch round the outline of each of the four heart shapes.

12 Replace the embellished squares in your arrangement and re-arrange as necessary.

Join Your Patches

13 Using a ¼" seam, join the squares together one row at a time.

> **Technique:** Basic Patchwork   >

14 Press the seam allowances in opposite directions to reduce bulk, i.e. Press the first row seam allowances to the right, the second row to the left and so on.

> **Technique:** Pressing for a Professional Finish   >

15 Pin row 1 to row 2 ensuring that all vertical seams are lined up.

16 Place a pin through each seam at 90 degrees to the raw edges.

> **Note:**
> Sewing over pins isn't as scary as it sounds, provided you slow down as you approach each pin. If the needle should hit a pin at a slow speed it is likely to slide off, but if it hits at a high speed it is likely to break the needle, or pin, or both.

17 Join the rows, leaving the pins in place, ensuring that all the seams match.

> **Note:**
> It is important to check that all your raw edges are lined up before stitching and you have stitched leaving a generous ¼" seam allowance on all edges. If there are any narrow seam allowances, these are likely to fray through to the front of the quilt after a few washes.

18 Press all horizontal seams open.

19 Give the whole block a thorough steam press, back and front ensuring all seam allowances are pressed as detailed above.

Add Your Border

20 Stitch together the short ends of the 5" strips, mixing up the different colours to your liking.

21 Press the seam allowances open.

22 Wrong sides together, pin a length of the 5" border to one of the long sides of your block. Trim the border top and bottom edges level with the patchwork panel.

23 Stitch in place. Open out border and press seam allowance towards the border.

24 Repeat with the other long side of the block.

25 Repeat with the top and bottom of the block.

26 Press the whole block and attached borders thoroughly.

Quilt Your Work

Technique: Basic Machine Quilting   >
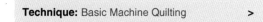

27 Iron backing fabric and lay out on a flat surface wrong side up.

28 Lay wadding on top and quilt top on top of that, right side up.

Tip: Selecting and Using Wadding   >
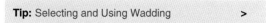

29 Smooth the quilt top over the wadding (you may wish to press it again first).

30 Insert two long quilting pins crosswise at each point where four large squares meet, beginning in the centre and smoothing the fabric as you go.

31 Placing the pins 4" apart and at right angles to the seam joining the border to the main block, pin all round the border

32 Using a 3mm straight stitch and quilting thread, and a walking foot if you have one, stitch in-the-ditch all round the border seam, smoothing the fabrics apart as you go to help the stitching sink into the seam.

33 Using quilting thread, sew on a button at each point where four squares intersect.

Technique: Basic Hand Sewing   >
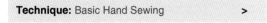

Bind it All Together

34 Join all the 4" squares together, ensuring that similar colours and tones are not placed together.

35 Press all the seam allowances in one direction

36 Fold the long strip of 4" squares in half lengthways and press.

37 Line up the end of your binding strip with the top of one long edge of the quilt, raw edges together, and pin.

38 Pin the strip along the entire length of the long edge and trim flush with the quilt edge.

39 Repeat with the other long edge.

40 Creating a ¼" seam, stitch the binding strip to the quilt (line your presser foot up with the raw edges).

Technique: Binding Edges   >

41 Flip the binding strip over to cover the raw edges and press.

42 Fold the strip over to the back of the quilt until the folded edge meets the stitching.

43 Press and pin in place.

44 Now add binding to the two short edges of the quilt, leaving an extra 1" at each end and ensuring the binding on the long edges stays folded in place.

45 Flip binding over as before.

46 To make perfect corners, turn in the extra 1" of binding towards the centre of the short edges and press.

47 Fold the binding over to meet the stitching as before and press and pin in place.

48 Using quilting thread and small, neat hand stitches, stitch the binding in place all around the quilt, paying particular attention to the corners.

Technique: Basic Hand Sewing   >

... and you're done.

53

Part 3: Basic Sewing Techniques

Simple techniques you will need to master for the sewing projects.

Accurate Measuring

Whatever sewing project you choose to tackle, you will need to measure accurately, which is not always as simple as it sounds.

What is the "right" and "wrong" side?

In these, and other, instructions, you may see the phrase "fold right sides together", or similar.

The "right" side of the fabric refers to the side that will be on show in the finished item you are making.

In commercial patterned fabrics it is usually clear which side of the fabric is designed for show and which is the reverse or "wrong" side. In other fabrics it may not be so clear so you must decide which side is going to be the "right" side and ensure you always use that as the right side.

Ironing Your Fabric

In order to measure accurately, your fabric must lie absolutely flat. To ensure this you may need to press it thoroughly to remove any creases, crumpling or folds.

The Right Tool for the Job

There are several tools you might wish to buy to enable you to measure accurately.

Tape Measures

Suitable for:

- taking body measurements
- measuring uneven surfaces

Rulers

Suitable for:

- rough measuring of fabric (using a 1m ruler)
- short measurements (using a 1ft/30cm ruler)

Acrylic Quilting Rulers and Squares

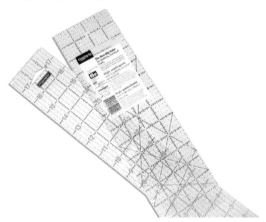

Although the initial cost of these rulers may seem high, they are absolutely invaluable, not just for any patchwork project that requires accurate

measuring and cutting, but also for any project that requires the cutting of several large pieces at a time such as bags and cushions. Once you get the hang of measuring and cutting with a quilter's ruler/square and rotary cutter, you can forget all that messing about with chalk and scissors and your sewing life will become a whole lot easier and a whole lot more accurate.

Quilter's rulers and squares are suitable for:

- accurate measuring and cutting fabric squares or lengths
- accurate measuring of angled pieces

Quilter's rulers and squares are generally marked in Imperial units but they are also now available with metric measurements too. The Imperial ones are usually marked 1", ½", ¼" and $\frac{1}{8}$".

Measure Twice, Cut Once

It's as true for sewing as it is for carpentry. Always make sure that your measurement is correct before cutting and measure twice (to be sure, to be sure). This will ensure you don't waste or ruin your fabric.

I cannot stress how important it is to line up your fabric with the correct marks and cut as accurately as you can. 1/8" may not sound very much, but if you are cutting a number of squares for a quilt or cushion and they are all 1/8" out, that can add up to quite an error!

Measuring Large Items

If you are going to be making large items such as cushions, quilts, curtains and blinds, it really is useful to invest in a 20 ½" quilter's square and metre rule. The combination of these two tools will make it much easier to square off large cushions and patchwork panels and will make cutting curtain and blind panels a breeze.

By lining one of the edges of the large square with a known straight edge, e.g. the selvedge of length of fabric, and laying the metre rule along the top edge, you will be able to slide the ruler back and forth while keeping it flush with the square.

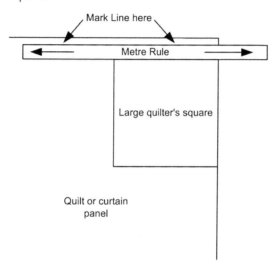

This will allow you to draw accurate lines across most of your fabric. If the piece is particularly wide and the ruler won't reach all the way across, simply move the square to the opposite side of the fabric, with the rule on top, and continue your line.

Rotary Cutting

Always use a Rotary Cutter and a Quilter's Square or Ruler when cutting fabric into strips or squares. This will give a professional finish to your project.

What is a 'Fat Quarter'?

You may see 'Fat Quarters' of fabric for sale in the shops. These are rough squares of fabric, generally for patchwork use, produced by cutting a metre (or a yard) of length of a roll of fabric.

Rolls of fabric are typically 40 to 45 inches wide, depending on the manufacturer. The resultant strip of fabric (either 1 m or 1 yrd long by 40 to 45 inches wide) is then cut into four to create four Fat Quarters.

The minimum dimensions for a Fat Quarter should therefore be 18 x 20 inches), allowing you to get nine 6 x 6 inch squares for your patchwork. The edges are often not cut straight and will need 'squaring up' with a Rotary Cutter and Ruler.

Similarly, 'Fat Eighths' are half this size (18 x 10 inches).

Watch it on YouTube

I have made some videos that will show you the ease of cutting with a rotary cutter. These are available on my website at www.time4me-workshops.co.uk/tips.htm and on YouTube

> **Video:** Preparing Shirts for Quilt Making   **>**

There are four videos on *Preparing Shirts for Quilt Making*.

- Cutting the Shirt into Useable Parts
- Cutting Quilting Squares from Short Backs
- Cutting Quilting Squares from Shirt Sleeves
- Cutting Quilting Squares from Shirt Fronts

For Rotary Cutting -You Will Need

- A large table or flat surface
- A large Cutting Mat
- A Rotary Cutter (45mm)
- A large non-slip Quilter's Square (20.5" x 20.5") or Ruler (24" x 6")

Cutting Accurately

Prepare Your Fabric

First, iron your fabric so that it lies perfectly flat. Then lay your ironed fabric on the cutting board, ready for cutting.

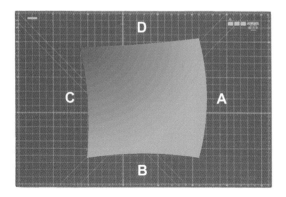

Position Your Quilter's Square/Ruler

Place your Quilter's Square or Ruler with the bottom right-hand corner at the bottom right-hand corner of the fabric, lining up the edges as closely as you can. Place your left-hand flat on the ruler, palm down to hold it in place (unless you are left-handed in which case you may wish to reverse these instructions).

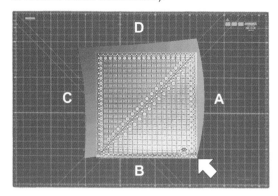

Release the Blade Guard on the Rotary Cutter

Release the blade guard on your Rotary Cutter to expose the blade. Depending on the manufacturer and type of cutter you have, this may be done either by sliding the guard back or squeezing the guard release handle.

Note:
Every time you lay your cutter down, ensure that you put the guard on. Rotary cutter blades are very sharp and, if you inadvertently pick up your cutter by the wrong end, it is very painful.

Make Your First Cut (A)

Place the Rotary Cutter blade on the fabric at the bottom right-hand corner of the square and stand immediately behind the line you are about to cut (away from your body). Place your index finger on the ridged area above the blade. Roll the blade forward smoothly along the side of the ruler, ensuring you maintain contact with it. Keep the cutter at an angle of 45 degrees, as shown in the diagram, and maintain downward pressure on the fabric at all times. Always cut away from your body.

Ease the Fabric Away

When you have made your first cut DO NOT MOVE THE RULER but ease the raw edge of the cut fabric away from the cut. If the fabric has not cut cleanly, you will need to repeat the cut.

Note:
Some fabrics such as raw silk or satin rarely cut cleanly the first time and may need several attempts. If you continue to have problems, sharpen or change your blade.

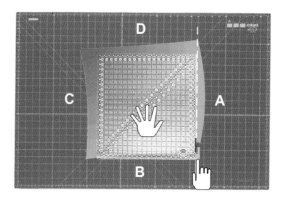

Rotate the Fabric and Make Your Second Cut (B)

Remove the square from the fabric and rotate the fabric 90° anti-clockwise so the edge you have just cut becomes the top edge. Line this edge up with one of the horizontal lines on the cutting mat. Replace the square on the fabric, lining up the top edge with the edge you have just cut. Then cut your second edge as shown at B in the diagram below. All of your other cuts can now be measured accurately from these straight edges.

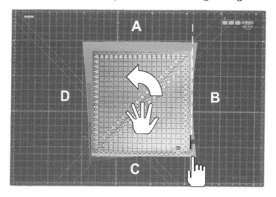

Measure Your Patchwork Strip

Turn your fabric 180° clockwise and position the 5-inch mark on your Ruler/Square over the straight edges. The right-hand edge of your Square/Ruler is the edge against which you are going to cut.

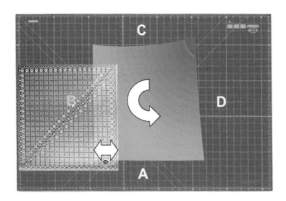

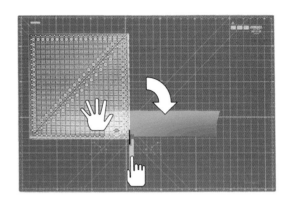

Cut Your Patchwork Strip

> **Note:**
> For consistency, the following steps are shown using the large square, but a smaller square or ruler, if you have one, is probably more practical for smaller pieces.

Again, place the Rotary Cutter blade on the fabric at the bottom right-hand corner of the square and roll the blade forward smoothly along the side of the ruler, cutting a 5" wide strip of fabric. If the fabric is slightly longer than the square, just keep on cutting to the end of the fabric.

Repeat for More Squares

Repeat until you have the required number of patchwork squares. You should be able to get three 5 x 5" squares easily from each strip, and get nine, or even sixteen, 5 x 5"squares from the entire Fat Quarter.

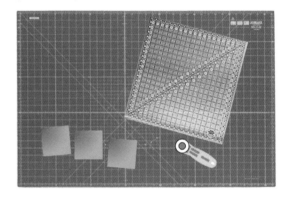

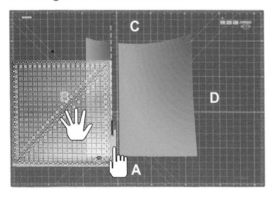

Cut Your Patchwork Square

Set aside the remainder of the fabric and turn the strip of fabric 90° clockwise. Place the 5" mark on your Square/Ruler over the previously cut edge and cut a 5" square.

Pressing for a Professional Finish

The single most important process with patchwork, in fact, with most sewing projects, is pressing. Proper pressing will give your finished work a professional appearance.

What is Pressing?

When we iron clothes at home, we move the iron soleplate across the fabric to smooth out creases. However, when pressing patchwork, we want to put creases in (by getting seam allowances to lie flat) rather than taking them out. To achieve this, the iron should be placed on the seam to be pressed for a few seconds and then lifted. Moving the soleplate across the piece can distort the seams and move seam allowances out of place.

However beautifully sewn your blocks are, if their seams are not pressed correctly, and in the right directions, your piece will never look truly finished.

Finger Pressing

If your seam allowances are proving a little difficult to separate with the edge of the iron, it is a good idea to separate and 'press' them with your fingertips first. Finger pressing is also useful in projects where a hard, pressed edge would be unsightly, such as in blind or curtain-making.

What Type of Iron should I Use?

For cotton fabrics a hot, steam iron is invaluable as is an ironing board with a thick padded cover. For this sort of pressing, a good iron is essential. Buy one with the highest wattage you can afford. Forget about rechargeable, cordless irons or ones that claim to have an Auto-off function. You will spend most of your time waiting for them to heat up and the rest of your time dabbing leaks and watermarks off your work.

If you are seriously into sewing and particularly patchwork, you may like to consider buying an iron with a steam generator. These are expensive, need a little more maintenance than a standard iron, but once you have tried one you won't be happy with anything else.

Whatever you do, don't succumb to a 'value' brand iron, they will never get hot enough, are liable to leak all over your work and, with the money spent replacing them, a dozen times, you could have bought a decent one.

Successful Pressing

Before you press any of the seams in your project it is important to make sure your iron is on the correct temperature for the fabric you are using. If in doubt, always err on the side of cooler rather than hotter as a hot iron on a delicate or synthetic fabric could cause irreversible damage.

Once you have pressed a seam, the piece should always be left to cool on the ironing board before moving on to the next seam. If the piece is moved while still hot, the seam allowances will not maintain their creases and you may introduce more creases where you don't want them.

Pressing Seams Open

If your seams are a little fiddly, try flattening them out with your fingers or the point of the iron soleplate. Once open, give them a good steam press and leave to cool.

Pressing Seams to One Side

When pressing seams to one side, lay the piece on the ironing board, hold it in place with the tip of the iron while you stretch it slightly with your left hand. Move the iron up the piece slowly, pressing the seam allowances to the left. Allow to cool. Pressing in this way helps to avoid a little ledge forming on the right side of the seam.

Getting a Good Finish on Thick Fabrics

If you find the fabrics you are using are thicker than standard patchwork cotton (such as furnishing fabrics) and unwilling to lie flat, a beechwood tailor's pressing block (or point presser) is a useful aid.

This is applied to the seam allowances as soon as the iron is removed, while the steam is still rising, and held in place until the seam is cooled and the steam has dissipated.

If the fabric finish allows it, it is a good idea to press on the right side as well.

Always remember to allow the piece to cool before removing it from the ironing board.

Basic Hand-Sewing

Many people claim to be hopeless at hand sewing, but it is an easy and useful skill to learn and can give the perfect finishing touch to many projects.

What is Hand Sewing?

Hand sewing falls into two basic categories – temporary and permanent.

Temporary stitches, which are sometimes referred to as 'tacking' or 'basting', are used for:

- marking fabrics where tailor's chalk is inappropriate
- holding layers of fabrics together ready for stitching, i.e. before quilting or stitching seams in dressmaking

Permanent stitches can be used to:

- finish edges and details i.e., bindings on quilts and cushions.
- pleat, tuck or gather fabrics i.e., on cushion fronts or garments
- make invisible hems
- decorate i.e. blanket stitch, buttonhole stitch and cross-stitch

Most Used Temporary Stitches

Even Basting

This is the most used of all temporary stitches and is found most commonly in dressmaking to hold together two edges, which are going to form a main seam, particularly in a close fitting garment.

It can also be used for easing a longer layer onto a shorter layer, such as when inserting sleeves into a garment or gathering a skirt onto a waistband.

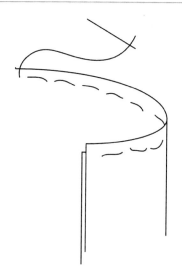

To make an even-basting seam:

1. Place the right sides of the fabric, to be joined, together and sew a line of running stitches which are equal in length on both sides of the seam and no longer than ¼".

2. If joining a gathered or pleated piece to a shorter piece, gather or pleat the section first and then baste to the second piece.

Uneven Basting

This type of basting is used for marking fabric, tacking hems and securing seams that don't need to be very strong. It is particularly useful in quilting where the long top stitch provides more anchorage than the bottom stitch, so holding the top layers more effectively.

To make an uneven basting seam:

1　Anchor the thread with a knot or back stitch, then make a short stitch of 1/8" – ¼" on the underside of the fabric.

2　Now make a stitch of ¼" – 1" on the top side.

3　Continue so the stitches on the top side of the fabric are 2 to 3 times as long as those on the underside.

Lap Basting

Here's a useful basting stitch for when you're planning to stitch bias seams that will be stretched during stitching. Standard basting would be inflexible and is likely to snap when stretched under the sewing machine.

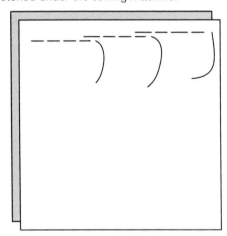

To lap-baste a bias seam:

1　Tie a knot at the end of your thread and even-baste for 6". Cut thread, leaving a 2" tail.

2　Repeat, starting at a point that overlaps the last few stitches and with a 2" tail instead of a knot.

3　Continue in this way for the remainder of the seam line and secure with a few backstitches.

Most Used Permanent Stitches

Running Stitch

A collection of small, even stitches that is used for seams that do not need to be very strong such as in garment linings or pockets. This is useful in areas where machine stitching accurately is difficult.

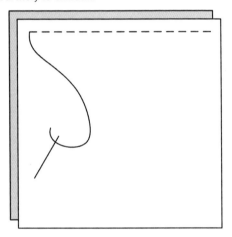

For running stitch:

1　Secure the thread with a knot or a few small backstitches.

2　Then take a few small stitches onto the needle of about 1/8" long and pull through.

3　Continue for length required.

Back Stitch

This is one of the strongest and most useful of permanent hand stitches as it looks just like machine stitching. This makes it useful for quick repairs when you don't want to get the machine out.

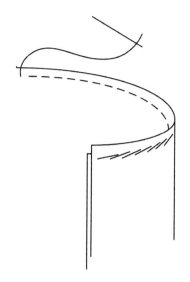

To make a back stitch seam:

1   Secure the thread with a knot or a few small backstitches, and then make a 1/8" stitch and pull the thread fully through the fabric.

2   Now insert the needle 1/16" to 1/8" behind where the thread exits the cloth and pull out again 1/8" in front of the stitch.

3   Insert the needle again at the end of the previous stitch and continue like this to the end of the seam.

Slip Stitch

This is the stitch we use most often when securing the binding on quilts, tablemats and wall hangings. It is used primarily to join two layers from the right side of the fabric and is also used extensively in hemming.

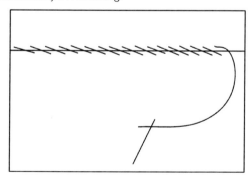

To slip stitch one layer over another:

1   Tie a knot in the thread and then insert the needle under edge of the top layer and pull through, hiding the knot underneath.

2   Pick up a small stitch (¼" to ½" ahead of where the needle exits the top layer) on the bottom layer.

3   Insert the needle in the folded edge of the top layer directly opposite the stitch just made and pull through.

4   Continue this way until the top layer is secure and pull the thread tight but not tight enough to cause puckering or breakage.

Sewing on Buttons

Sewing on a button is one of those things that we assume everyone can do, but just in case you haven't done one in a while, here's a reminder.

Sewing on Buttons with Holes

1   Using tailor's chalk, mark the point where the button is to be attached.

2   Cut a long length of strong, toning thread, thread it through your needle. Pull the thread through until the ends meet and knot securely.

3   Insert your needle into the fabric from the back and pull it through until the knot is resting against the fabric.

4   Slip the button over the needle and hold it against the fabric with your other hand.

5   If the button is of the two-hole variety, pass your needle down through the second hole, and then up through the first hole. Repeat approximately six times. Don't pull the thread too tight or you won't be able to get the button through the buttonhole, but be careful not to leave any thread loops.

6   If your button is of the four-hole variety, repeat the above for the second set of holes.

7   Pass the needle through to the back of the fabric and then, several times, through the stitches you've made to secure.

8   Snip off the thread.

Sewing on a Button with a Shank

1   Mark the point where the button is to be attached and thread your needle as before.

2   Bring the needle up through the back of the fabric.

3   Pass the needle through the wire loop or shank of the button then down through the fabric. Bring the needle back to the right side of the fabric then repeat approximately six times. Don't pull the thread too tight and but be careful not to leave any thread loops.

4   Now wrap the thread tightly around the stitches you have made, just below the wire loop or shank, approximately six times.

5   Pass the thread through to the back of the fabric and then, to secure, several times through the stitches you've made.

6   Snip off the thread.

Creating Appliqué Designs

There are numerous methods of appliqué, some simpler than others, which can be used to bring even your simplest projects to life.

What is Appliqué?

Appliqué is simply the laying and fixing of one piece of fabric over another to create a design. All sorts of fabrics can be used for appliqué and even just the addition of a few simple shapes such as leaves, hearts or something seasonal, can make all the difference to a plain project.

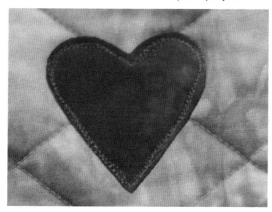

The easiest way to create appliqué designs is to fuse or bond the appliqué to the project surface and then stitch in place. Fusing or bonding a fusible web to the appliqué fabric will stabilize it, meaning you can use a whole range of fabrics, and will also seal the raw edges, minimizing any fraying on even the loosest-weave fabrics.

Some Appliqué Images

You can download some appliqué template images from my website using the following link.

Tip: Ideas for Appliqué	>

Alternatively, you can make your own appliqué template using royalty-free clipart.

Fusible Webs

Fusible web, also known as 'Bondaweb' (or 'Wonderunder' in the US) 'Therm'a'Bond' or 'Steam-a-Seam', is essentially a sheet of fabric adhesive in the form of a dry mesh, with either one or two paper backings to enable easy handling and application. Applying heat to the fusible web, by ironing, melts the glue to allow you to stick one fabric to another, when correctly positioned.

Some brands of fusible web are designed for 'no-sew' projects and you may find these make your fabric a little stiff. They may also cause beads of glue on your sewing machine needle if you do decide to stitch through them. Some, like Steam-a-Seam are pressure-sensitive, so you can temporarily fix your design in place to see how it looks before ironing it on permanently. So make sure you choose the grade and brand that is suitable for your particular project.

Remember that the finished appliqué will be a mirror image of the original image so if you want to use letters and numbers in your design you may need to use a product such as Steam-a-Seam. As this has two paper backings either side of the glue sheet, you can trace your image onto one paper backing, then turn over and trace through onto the other backing. When you remove a backing to press the glue onto the fabric, you will need to ensure that you keep the glue sheet (which can be adhered to either backing) with the backing that has the mirror image of the finished appliqué you want on your project.

Adding an Appliqué Image Using Fusible Web

To add an appliqué image to your project:

1   Find a suitable image. It is best to start with a simple shape such as a heart or circle until you get used to the technique.

2   Trace the image onto a piece of fusible web. If the original is faint, you may need to use a light box or hold it up against a window.

3   Cut the image out roughly.

4   Set your iron to the wool setting and switch off the steam.

> **Note:**
> If you are planning to do a lot of appliqué, it is a good idea to keep a separate iron and small ironing board just for this purpose. Little bits of glue frequently get stuck to the iron and it can be very annoying when dirty glue marks end up on the front of a recently completed quilt top. If you don't have a separate iron, use a piece of thin cotton or polycotton as a pressing cloth and turn your iron up a notch or two.

5   Place the appliqué fabric face down on the ironing board and iron flat.

6   If you have used Steam-a-Seam, remove one of the paper backings at this point, ensuring that the glue sheet remains with the drawn image.

7   Place the image, glue side down on the rear of the fabric.

8   Press, the iron over the image and hold for 5-10 seconds. Don't be tempted to move the iron around as this may cause the paper backing to move and leave glue smears on the iron and fabric.

9   Check if the image is properly adhered to the fabric.

10   Allow the adhered image and fabric to cool completely.

11   Cut carefully around the image.

12   If you have used Steam-a-Seam, peel off the paper backing and finger-press your image in place on your project until you are happy with the position.

13 If you have used another fusible web, pin or use low-tack sticky tape to temporarily fix your image.

14 Once you are happy with the position, remove the paper backing and press with the iron as before.

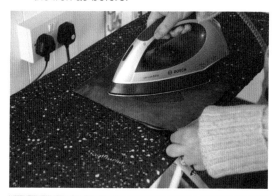

Note:
If, when you attempt to remove the paper backing, the glue starts peeling away from the fabric, press as before, cool, and try again.

Once your images are bonded in place, you need to consider what kind of stitching you are going to use to secure the edges. Many people choose satin stitch, but I find this can overpower the image and anything less than perfect stitching will be noticed.

I find that a medium-width zig-zag or blanket stitch is ideal for simple shapes or home-style-type images. If you are confident using free-motion embroidery, this is ideal for securing appliqué and is great for more complex shapes such as leaves, flowers, fruit and vegetables and landscapes.

Make the Most of Frayed Edges

You can really make a feature of frayed edges in appliqué and this works particularly well using hand-dyed fabrics rather than commercially printed ones. In dyed fabrics, the dye is suffused through the entire fabric, meaning the edges are just as vibrant as the surface, while in the printed fabrics, the edges can be a bit dull with the colour only appearing on a fraction of the threads.

Hide Edges with Freezer Paper

If you prefer your edges to be hidden, you could use freezer paper appliqué.

Freezer paper was originally produced as a food wrapping but one day, some clever quilter realised that if you ironed the waxy side onto fabric, it would stick, albeit temporarily, but long enough to make it useful for appliqué. It is now readily available from quilt shops and quilting suppliers.

Note:
The only disadvantage of using freezer paper for appliqué is that the paper has to be removed after the image is stitched on to the background. This means either leaving a gap in the stitching and pulling the paper out before completion or making a slit in the background fabric behind the image to remove the paper.

Adding an Appliqué Image Using Freezer Paper

1   Trace your pattern onto the non-waxy side of the freezer paper.

Note:
Remember that the finished appliqué will be a mirror image of the original image. If you don't want a mirror image, then trace the image onto the shiny side of the freezer paper. Instead of ironing the shiny side of the paper onto your fabric, place the waxy side down and use the shiny side to secure the folded fabric edges and to temporarily bond the appliqué to the background.

2   Cut out the image and iron it onto the back of your chosen fabric.

3   Cut around the template leaving a ¼" (6mm) border for turning.

4   Turn the fabric edges in as neatly as possible, clipping any curves as necessary and press in place.

5   Pin the appliqué in place or use a little temporary spray fixative to hold it in place.

6   Use a narrow zig-zag or blind hemming stitch to secure. If you want to remove the freezer paper without cutting into the background fabric, leave a small gap in your stitching and pull out the paper using tweezers or small pliers.

7   Otherwise, using small, sharp scissors, cut a slit in the background fabric, behind the appliqué, and carefully remove the paper.

8   Press lightly but do not completely flatten the appliqué against the background fabric as this could ruin the relief effect.

Finishing Edges

There are various ways to deal with edges to ensure that your fabrics don't fray, are adequately secured and look neat. Here's an overview of some of the ways I use.

Fabric Edges

Selvedges

A 'selvedge' is the finished edge of a length of fabric. It is usually white and printed with details of the manufacturer, the name of the design and the colours used in the design. These edges, being firm and woven, need no further finishing.

Raw Edges

A 'raw edge' is the cut edge of a piece of fabric. Some fabrics are more prone to fraying than others but most will show some signs of fraying when washed. If you do not intend to use this to decorative effect, it is a good idea, and gives a professional-looking finish, to give your raw edges one of the following treatments.

Overlocking

If you have an overlocker, and know how to use it, this is the best possible way to finish off a raw edge, particularly one that is likely to be seen as in an unlined jacket or coat. It is beyond the scope of this book to give instruction on using overlockers, but it is well worth spending some time studying your user manual and getting to grips with the threading and tension.

Zig-zagging

If you have an 'overlocking' stitch on your sewing machine, this is the next best thing to an actual overlocker. Otherwise, select a full width zig-zag stitch at a stitch length of 1.5-2mm and use this to finish of your edges.

Straight Stitch

If you are using an elderly sewing machine or an industrial model which doesn't have a zig-zag facility, you can stop serious fraying by working a row of straight stitches about 2-3mm from the cut edge.

Pinking

If you don't have any other method of finishing your edges, a pair of pinking shears will stop fraying for a while. But a few washes will soon wear down the points made by the shears and some fraying is inevitable.

Bound Edges

This is a method which was commonly used in tailored suits and jackets but has recently seen a revival on the high street in the form of floral-bound seam allowances in lightweight casual jackets. It is very useful for adding a quirky and functional finish to your home dressmaking.

Fray Reduction Spray

This is a method commonly used by those who prefer not to use fusible web in appliqué. It is not a method I've tried, but can be useful if you are using a very loose weave fabric.

Hems

Hems are the classic way to finish off the lower edges of clothing and the edges of pockets etc.

Single Hems

Single hems are useful on items which are made of a fabric which would be too thick and heavy if doubled over, but they do need to be used in conjunction with a method of edge finishing such as overlocking or zig-zagging.

Single hems are also popular on lightweight dresses, trousers and skirts and also on special occasion wear such as ball gowns and bridesmaid dresses. They are almost always used with overlocked edges.

Double-Hems

Double hems are commonly used if a firm edge is required on a household item such as an apron or the button band or envelope edge of a cushion back. If a double hem is used, it is not usually necessary to pre-finish the raw edge.

Double hems are also commonly used on the lower edges of formal skirts, dresses and trousers where they are hand-stitched or, in commercial clothing, blind-stitched in place.

Binding Edges

This is a great way to finish off quilts and wall hangings. There are several different variants depending on the type of edge you're finishing off.

Choosing a Binding

Choosing a suitable binding is as important as choosing fabrics for the rest of the quilt. A weak or pale-coloured binding can seem out of place on a strong coloured quilt as the edges may lack definition making the whole thing seem unbalanced.

It can be a good idea to use one of the fabrics that features in the main body of your quilt top. If you have used stripes in your design, you could try using the same fabric with the stripes cut at right angles to the quilt edge.

Whatever you decide to do, do spend time trying out various options and auditioning various fabrics for your binding before you make the first cut. It is tempting to rush through this stage just to get the project finished, but take your time and you will be rewarded with a quilt you can be proud of.

Types of Binding

There are two main types of binding that I use in my workshops. These are:

- **Straight binding** – This type of binding, which is cut on the grain of the fabric, is the most commonly used on decorative quilts and wall-hangings with straight edges. Straight binding can be used with lapped or mitred corners. Using the mitred corners method involves using a strip of binding that is long enough to go all the way around your project. Popular with many quilters as it is easy to do but, in my opinion, not nearly as neat as lapped corners.

- **Bias-binding** – This type of binding, which is cut on the bias, or diagonal of the fafabric, is very useful when you want to bind curved edges or around corners. This type of binding can be useful in quilts which are going to be subjected to a lot of use and frequent washing as there are many threads in the edge of the binding rather than just the one or two in a straight binding. Commercial bias-binding is too loosely woven to be suitable for quilt edgings.

As a rule of thumb I like to cut bindings for cushions, 2" (5cm) wide and quilts up to lap size, 3" (7.5cm) wide. Anything larger than this, I think looks better with a wider 4" (10cm) binding. I always make bindings double as I feel a single thickness can be a little insubstantial and can be prone to rippling, whereas a double thickness provides a strong, firm edge.

Making Straight Binding with Lapped Corners

To make your own binding:

1 Measure all round your project and add 6" for seam allowances and corners.

2 If your chosen binding fabric is wide enough to reach across the longest side of your project, cut four strips (of your chosen size) across the width of the fabric.

3 If your fabric is not wide enough, then calculate how many strips you will need to cut (of the width of the fabric) to reach round your project, including seam allowances and corners.

4 If you had to cut a number of shorter strips, join all of these together by their short edges and press the seams open.

5 Take your strip or strips, fold them in half lengthways, wrong sides together, and press.

6 If you have four strips, pin one each of the strips to opposite sides of your project, raw edges together.

7 If you have one long strip, measure and cut pieces just long enough to fit two opposite sides of your project.

8 Pin in place, raw edges together.

9 Stitch the strips using ¼" seam allowance.

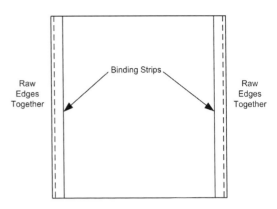

10 Now flip the stitched binding strips over and press.

11 Fold over to the wrong side so the folded edge meets the row of stitching. Press and pin in place.

12 Add two more binding strips to the remaining edges but this time leave an overhang of 1" (2.5cm) at each end.

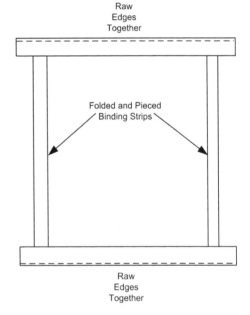

13 Now flip the stitched binding strips over and press.

14 Turn the project over and fold the 1" overhang in towards the centre of the strip at each end.

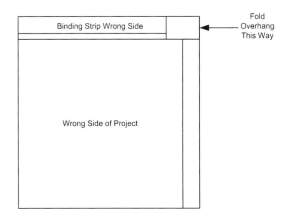

15 Now fold over the entire binding strip so the folded edge meets the line of stitching. Press and pin in place.

16 Stitch in place with small neat hand-stitches, paying particular attention to the corners.

Making Straight Binding with Mitred Corners

To make straight binding with mitred corners:

1 Measure all round your project and add 6" (15cm) for joining.

2 Cut enough strips (on the straight grain of the fabric) to make up a strip of the measurement taken above.

3 Join all the strips together by their short sides and press the seams open.

> **Note:**
> It is always a good idea to start this type of binding on the bottom edge of a quilt or wall hanging. This means the join will be less obtrusive and that you will have a continuous strip of binding all round the top and sides. This will lessen the possibility of the quilt edges rippling if they are hung up.

4 Starting at the centre of the bottom edge of your project, pin the binding to the edge, raw edges together, leaving a tail of 3" (7.5cm) for joining.

5 Calculate what the finished width of your binding will be i.e. when it is stitched on and turned over to the back of the project.

6 Start stitching the binding on, starting where you began pinning, and finishing the width of the finished binding from the corner. For example, if the finished width of the binding is 1", stop stitching 1" from the corner. Finish with a few reverse stitches.

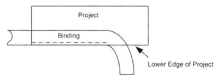

7 Now fold the binding strip away from the corner as shown in the diagram, and pin in place.

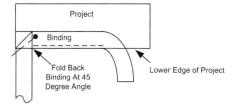

8 Fold the binding back towards the quilt as shown and pin along the side of the quilt.

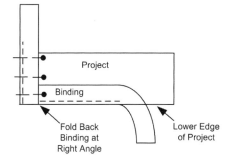

9 Place the sewing machine foot about ½" (1cm) from the corner, facing away from the corner and backstitch up to the corner.

10 Stitch the binding to the quilt side, completing the other mitres in the same way.

11 Continue stitching the binding round to the starting point, leaving a 3" (7.5cm) tail.

75

12 Open out both the 3" ends and join back to back. Pin and stitch.

13 Trim seam allowance and press.

14 Fold over binding to wrong side and stitch in place.

Making Bias Binding

To make your own bias binding:

1 Measure all round your project and add 6" (20cm) for joining.

2 Lay the ironed fabric out on a flat surface. To make bias strips you will need to start with a squared-off corner or fat quarter of the fabric you would like to use.

3 Fold over one corner diagonally to a depth of about 12-20" (30-50cm) so the edges of the fold are parallel with the edges of the fabric.

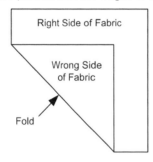

4 Lay a quilter's 24" ruler along the folded edge to the depth of your chosen binding size.

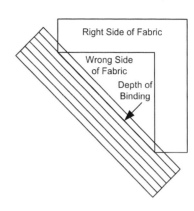

5 Carefully cut along the rule with a rotary cutter.

6 Open out the folded strip and cut in half along its length to form 2 strips of the same width.

7 Continue cutting strips in this manner (you won't have to cut them in half any more) until you have enough to reach around your project plus 6" (15cm).

8 To join the bias strips into one long strip, take two strips and lay them face up as shown in the diagram.

9 Now fold one strip over the other as shown below with the points overlapping

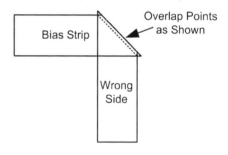

10 Stitch using a ¼" (1cm) seam.

11 Join all your bias strips together on the bias until you have one long strip.

12 Press seams open.

13 Fold the strip in half lengthways, wrong sides together, and press.

14 Apply to your project as shown in the individual instructions.

Making Piping

Piping adds a bit of luxury and smartness to an otherwise plain cushion and it's relatively easy to make.

Types of Piping

Piping can come in all shapes and sizes. You can buy it ready made in an array of different colours and fabrics or cords or you can make it yourself.

Piping on cushions is normally made from a long strip of bias cut fabric stitched around a length of cotton or polyester piping cord. This is available in a range of different thicknesses and you can choose the type depending on the size of your cushion and the effect you are looking for.

You can cover it in the same fabric as your cushion cover, which can look very stylish, or for something that will stand out more, choose a harmonising or contrasting fabric. A little of your curtain fabric around a plain cushion can really pull your look together.

You Will Need

- **Fabric – 1 x fat quarter should be sufficient for an 18" (45cm) – 20" (50cm) cover.**
- **Enough piping cord to reach all around the edge of your cushion pad with 4" (5cm) extra**

Piping a Standard Cushion Cover

Making Bias Strips

To make bias strips you will need to start with a squared-off corner or fat quarter of the fabric you would like to use.

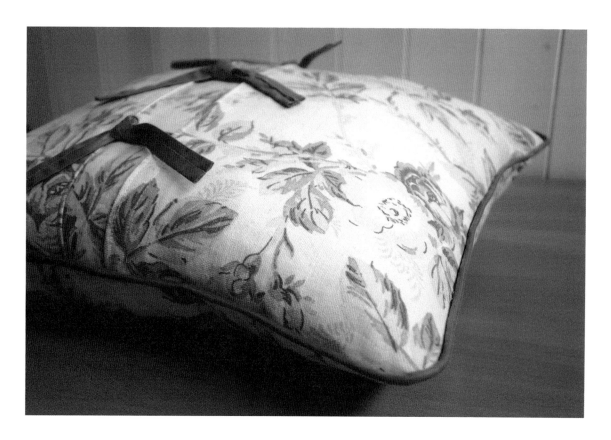

1   Lay the ironed fabric out on a flat surface.

2   Fold over one corner diagonally to a depth of about 12" so the edges of the fold are at right angles to the edges of the fabric.

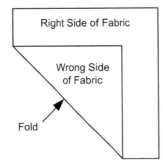

3   Lay a quilter's 24" ruler along the folded edge to a depth of 1 ½".

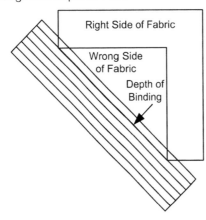

4   Carefully cut along the rule with a rotary cutter.

5   Open out the folded strip and cut in half along its length to form 2 strips of the same width.

6   Continue cutting strips in this manner until you have enough to reach around your cushion cover plus 6" (15cm).

Joining Bias Strips Together

7   To join the bias strips into one long strip, take two strips and lay them face up as shown in the diagram.

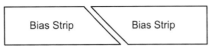

8   Now fold one strip over the other as shown below with the points overlapping

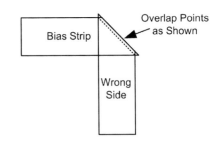

9   Stitch using a ¼" (1cm) seam.

10   Join all your bias strips together on the bias until you have one long strip.

11   Press seams open.

12   Fold your long bias strip in half lengthways, wrong sides together, and lay the piping cord inside against the fold. If the bias strip is longer than the cord, cut to the same length as the cord.

13   Fit a zipper foot to your sewing machine.

14   Place your folded piping under the machine foot with the piping cord butted up against the edge of the foot and stitch – using a 2.5mm stitch – the full length of the bias strip.

Attaching the Piping

15   Using a small round disc such as the lid of a box of pins, round off the corners of the front cushion panel using tailor's chalk to mark the line and trim with scissors.

16   Beginning midway on one of the long edges, pin your piping all the way round the right side of the front cushion panel, matching the raw edges together and leaving a tail of 2-3" at each end of the piping.

17   To join the two ends of the binding, unpick a few stitches so you can open out the fabric. Place the ends right side together, so the binding is a snug fit around the cushion panel edge, and stitch so the seam will lie flat.

18   Trim seam allowance to ½" and press open.

19 Trim the piping cord ends so they overlap each other by 1" approx. Cut off 1" approx from one of the three strands of each end of piping and 'knit' the remaining 4 ends together .

20 Fold over the seamed binding and pin in place.

21 With your zipper foot resting lightly against the piping cord (you will press it closer to the piping when stitching the cushion back on) stitch the binding to the cushion front panel.

22 Continue with cushion as required.

Adding Piping to Sofa Cushions

Adding piping to sofa or mattress style cushions, which have a gusset inserted between the top and bottom panels, is similar to adding it to standard cushions except that the piping will need to be applied to the top and bottom edges of the cushion before the gusset is added.

Adding Piping to Quilts

Extra interest and texture can be added to quilts and hangings by inserting a row of narrow piping in between the border and binding.

Zips in Cushion Covers

Many people avoid the Z-word, believing it to be full of hidden pitfalls that will put them off sewing forever. But once your master the simple technique of putting in a zip, it can open up a completely new world of projects.

Zips Types

Closing a cushion back with a zip is not the always the first choice of the novice stitcher but it does give a smooth finish and is a good choice for cushion covers that may need frequent washing.

Cushion zips can be inserted in a number of different positions depending on whether the cushion is intended to be double-sided (the zip is hidden and both sides of the cushion can be used) or single sided (where the zip is inserted in the centre back and only one side of the cushion is intended to be seen).

Choosing the Right Zip

For cushion covers, try to find a zip that matches the fabric or is slightly darker, rather than lighter. If your cushion cover is of a patterned fabric, try to match the background colour or choose a shade that is slightly darker.

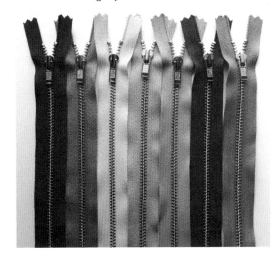

The zip should be a standard dressmaking nylon or plastic zip and should ideally be 2" (5cm) shorter than the bottom edge of the finished cover. If you have a nylon zip of the right colour that is too long, you can easily shorten it by sewing a few bar tacks over the teeth (using strong, doubled thread) at the correct length and snipping off the excess ½" (1.5cm) below the tacks.

Inserting a Zip in the Centre Back of a Cushion Cover

You may find it helpful to see my video on *How to Make a Cushion*.

Video: Zip Closure   **>**

This type of fastening is easy to insert and ideal for a first cushion project.

1 Place the two cushion back panels right sides together.

> **Note:**
> Zips are normally inserted in the centre cushion back but can be anywhere in the back panel.

2 Lay your zip centrally down one long edge, leaving a gap of approx 1" between the zip tapes and the edge of the fabric.

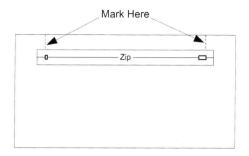

3 Using tailor's chalk, mark, on the cushion fabric, where the zip teeth begin and end.

4 Using a ½" seam stitch from the edge of the fabric to this mark.

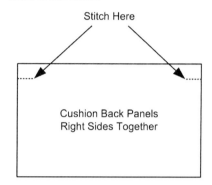

5 Press entire seam allowance open from one seam to the other.

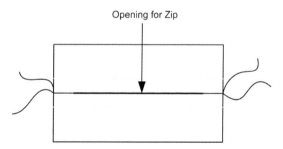

6 Turn over the joined panels and lay on a flat surface.

7 Place the zip in the opening between the folded edges of the seam allowances and pin the left-hand folded edge of the fabric close to the teeth of the zip.

8 Lap the right-hand edge slightly over the left-hand edge and pin in place, placing the pins against the teeth.

9 Tack all round the zip and remove the pins.

10 Fit a zipper foot onto your sewing machine and move the needle to the right side of the foot.

Note:
On some types of sewing machine, you may need to move the position of the foot rather than the needle.

11 Open the zip to a distance of 2". Beginning at the edge of the fabric nearest the top of the zip, stitch the left-hand side of the zip, ensuring you catch in the zip tapes, until you reach the zip pull, keeping the edge of the foot up against the teeth.

12 Stop the machine, place the needle in the fabric and raise the presser foot.

13 Close the zip, lower the presser foot and carry on stitching to the end of the fabric.

Note:
Don't be tempted to stitch around the bottom of the zip and up the other side. If you do this it is likely that the zip will appear slightly twisted and the top edges may not meet.

14 Move the needle to the left side of the foot and repeat the procedure above again keeping the foot up against the teeth.

Inserting a Zip in the Side-Seam of a Cushion Cover

Slightly trickier for the uninitiated, but once you've done it once, you'll never look back.

1 Fit a zipper foot to your sewing machine.

2 Place the front panel of the cushion cover face down on a flat surface.

3 Centre your zip, face down, along the bottom edge of the panel lining up the zip edge with the raw edge of the fabric.

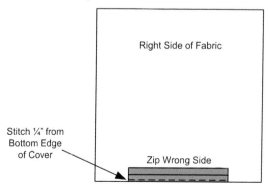

4   Stitch 1/2" (1.5cm) from the bottom edge of the cover, as close to the zip teeth as possible.

5   Now take the back panel of the cushion cover and lay it face down on top of the front, aligning the edges.

6   Starting at one side of the zip, stitch all round the cover, with a ½" seam allowance taking care not to catch the zip end tapes into the stitching.

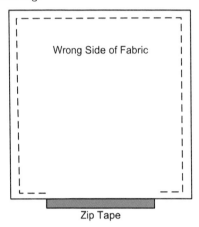

Note:
Before you start stitching the remaining edge of the zip to the back cushion panel, ensure that you open the zip a little way first. Otherwise, you will find it fiddly to open once stitched.

7   Carefully stitch the remaining side of the zip to the lower edge of the back cushion panel as close to the teeth as possible. Start at the lower end of the zip, stitch to within 2" (5cm) of the top of the sip, stop, place the needle in the fabric, lift the presser foot, open the zip past the needle and continue sewing to the top of the zip.

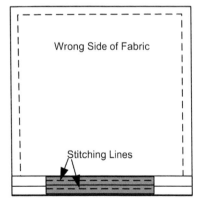

Making Buttonholes

Another scary subject that has been made incredibly simple by the advances in sewing machine technology. Many machines will now make perfect buttonholes at the touch of a button or two.

Types of Buttonhole

There are many different types of buttonholes, but they all fall into two main categories – worked or bound. The type of buttonhole that you choose for a particular project will depend on:

- The project or garment and what it will be used for.
- The fabric the project is made from
- Your sewing ability

Most of us automatically choose the sewing machine option. It's quick, easy (when you know how to do it) and every buttonhole is the same.

Worked Buttonhole

A worked buttonhole is essentially a slit in a piece of fabric (or garment) that is finished off with hand or machine stitches. A standard buttonhole has two sides of the same length, and two ends finished with bar tacks. Only machine-worked buttonholes are discussed in this skill sheet.

Anatomy of a Worked Buttonhole

A standard, machine-worked buttonhole is essentially made up of four parts, a left and right hand bead, which are normally worked in a narrow satin stitch, and a top and bottom bar tack, which are worked in a satin stitch the width of the two beads.

Usually a sewing machine, with an automatic buttonhole facility, will stitch a buttonhole in the following order:

- Left-hand bead
- Reverse straight stitch back to the top of the bead

- Top bar tack
- Right-hand bead
- Bottom bar tack

A worked buttonhole is always made through all the layers of fabric of a project or garment, including any interfacings, facings and backings. If you are intending to work buttonholes over a particular area, take care to make sure that all the layers are of a consistent colour to avoid any clashes when the buttonhole is cut open.

The main difference between hand and machine-worked buttonholes, is that hand-worked are slit and then stitched, while machine-worked are stitched and then slit. Hand worked buttonholes are not covered in this manual, which is primarily concerned with sewing-machine techniques, but details can be found in any good hand-sewing book.

Machine-Worked Buttonholes

The most commonly used worked buttonhole is the machine-worked buttonhole.

As there are so many different types of sewing machine available these days, it is outside the scope of this skill sheet to detail all the various methods of making machined buttonholes. Some machines are capable of one-step buttonholes and others of three-step buttonholes, depending on the model. Nevertheless, if you have an instruction manual, there is sure to be a mention of buttonholes somewhere in there and, if it is a modern machine, it is unlikely to be difficult.

Most sewing machines come supplied with a buttonhole foot and these can vary in construction and complexity.

Some sewing machines, again depending on the make and age have a balance control which can be used to make sure that both 'beads' of the buttonhole are the same tension. Check your instruction manual for its use.

Whichever buttonhole facility your sewing machine offers, it is advisable to place a piece of interfacing between the fabric and facing when working with stretchy, heavy-duty or loosely woven fabrics. This will prevent the buttonhole stretching or tearing during use.

It is always a good idea to make several test buttonholes before the real event. If you have any left over, use a piece of the fabric from your project, complete with interfacing.

Machined Buttonhole - Method

To make a machined buttonhole:

1   Mark the position of the buttonholes on your project, both starting point and length.

2   Referring to your instruction manual, fit the buttonhole foot to your sewing machine.

3   Set your machine to stitch a standard buttonhole. This may be a three or one-step

process depending on the make and age of the machine.

4   Stitch the buttonhole as directed by the instruction manual.

5   If your sewing machine does not finish off the threads, thread these through to the back of your work and tie off. Otherwise, snip the threads off at the front.

6   Take a small pair of sharp-pointed scissors or a seam ripper.

7   Starting at one end of the buttonhole slit, just inside the bar, cut the fabric as far as the centre point.

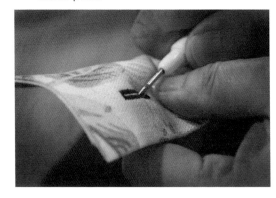

8   Repeat from the other end of the buttonhole slit so the two cuts meet in the centre.

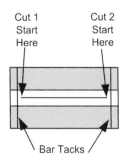

Basic Patchwork

Patchwork can be made using the smallest scraps of fabric and is ideal for using up leftovers from large projects.

Patchwork with Squares

A huge range of patchwork items can be made using just squares and rectangles and these can be a good choice if you have some small pieces of favourite fabrics to use up. As cotton fabrics are easy to cut and are not prone to stretching or fraying too badly, it is a good idea to start with these.

Accurate Cutting

Your fabrics should be cut using a rotary cutter and quilter's ruler. How accurate you need to be depends upon the sort of look you are after but if you are just beginning, I would recommend getting used to accurate cutting and piecing.

Technique: Rotary Cutting   >

Pressing

The single most important process with patchwork, and indeed with most sewing projects, is pressing.

Technique: Pressing for a Professional Finish   >

Patchwork Blocks

There a vast number of patchwork blocks to choose from and patterns and instructions for these can be found online, in craft books and in magazines. It is a good idea to stick to the simpler ones until you are happy with your cutting and stitching skills.

To Make a Simple Patchwork Block

1   Cut 16 x 4" (10cm) 100% cotton squares and arrange them into a pleasing design.

Technique: Rotary Cutting   >

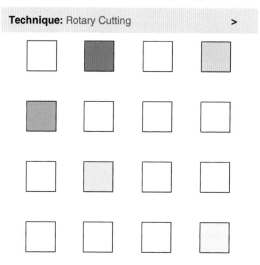

2   Take the first two squares from the first (top) row and place them right sides together.

3   Set your sewing machine for a straight stitch 2.5mm in length and fit a standard zig-zag foot.

4   Stitch the squares together down one side using a ¼" (6mm) seam. It is not necessary to do any reverse stitching at the beginning and end of the seam as these seam ends will

be stitched over when the rows are joined together.

Note:
Many sewing machine manufacturers produce a special patchworking foot whose edge is exactly ¼" (6mm) from the needle. If, like me, you are using a standard zig-zag foot, and you think your seam allowance is a little too wide and your machine has a facility to move the needle, you can always move the needle one or two notches to the right. The most important thing is to make all the seam allowances the same size.

5   Continue adding squares until all those from the top row are joined into a strip.

6   Repeat with the remaining rows.

7   Now using a hot steam iron, press all the seam allowances in row 1 to the left, slightly stretching the strip as you press. This helps to eliminate the little 'ledges' that can form on the right side seams.

8   Allow the strip to cool on the ironing board and then turn it over and press again, stretching it slightly and ensuring the seam allowances remain pressed in the same direction. Allow to cool.

9   Repeat with the other rows, pressing the seam allowances in row 2 to the right, row 3 to the left and row 4 to the right.

Press All Row 1 Seams
In This Direction
←

Press All Row 2 Seams
In This Direction
→

10   Now place row one face up and place row two on top, face down, lining up the vertical seams. You will find that pressing the seams in opposite directions means that they can now 'interlock' together.

11   Pin all the seams together placing the pins at 90 degrees through each seam.

12   Using a ¼" seam, stitch the two rows together, ensuring that the vertical seam allowances remain flat and in the direction in which they were pressed.

Note:
Sewing over pins isn't as scary as it sounds, provided you slow down as you approach each pin. If the needle should hit a pin at a slow speed, it is likely to slide off, but if it hits at a high speed, it is likely to break the needle, or pin, or both.

13   Using a hot, steam iron, carefully press the horizontal seam open, ensuring that the vertical seam allowances remain pressed in the correct directions.

14   Repeat with the remaining two rows.

15   When all the squares are joined together and the seams thoroughly pressed, turn the piece over and press again.

This piece can be used as a cushion front or as a starting square for a larger quilt.

Basic Machine Quilting

Machine quilting is quick, relatively easy and can add so much texture and definition to all sorts of projects from bags to cushions to quilts.

What is Machine-Quilting?

Machine quilting is not just a quicker way of quilting, than the traditional hand method, it also has properties, of its own, that make it the first choice for many quilters. It produces a stronger line than hand quilting and can be used to produce striking geometric designs, which can be further enhanced by the choice of threads.

Machine quilting can be carried out using a walking foot or you can also use a free-motion technique with a darning or embroidery foot. Some high-end machines also have a programmed stitch that simulates hand quilting. This is achieved by threading the top or bobbin path with an invisible nylon thread, which is used to make alternate stitches so that only the quilting thread is seen.

When is Quilting Required?

Quilting of a piece is usually advisable when you have three or more layers of fabric and wadding which are larger than 10" square. If you are quilting a quilt or throw, it is advisable to have quilted areas no more than 10" apart. This stops the layers coming apart, or 'bagging' in the unquilted areas. Of course, you don't have to quilt just because a piece needs it, you can quilt whatever and whenever you want – just because it looks good.

What Threads Should I Use?

Many books claim that you should use the same thread in the top and bottom of the machine when quilting. I have found that winding 100% cotton quilting threads and machine embroidery threads onto the bobbin (unless of course you are quilting from the back) can cause no end of problems. Quilting and embroidery threads, depending on the brand, can be very springy and positively unruly at times. I always advise my customers to use a good quality all-purpose polyester, toning thread in the bobbin.

Unless you can match your thread exactly with the colour of your quilt background, use a thread that is a shade darker rather than lighter as it is more likely to blend in. This is assuming of course, that you don't want your quilting to contrast with your fabric, if you do, and your fabric is multi-coloured, try picking one of the minor colours (in the fabric) as a quilting thread.

Machine-Quilting with a Walking Foot

A walking foot works by synchronising the feed dogs with the needle ensuring that the quilt top and backing are fed through the machine at the same rate. This is achieved by linking the foot to the needle motion by a forked structure (supplied already fitted to the foot) which rests on the screw that holds the needle in place.

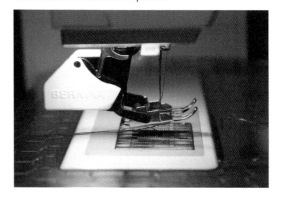

Walking feet are available for most popular sewing machines. Check in your instruction manual if one is mentioned for your particular model.

Walking feet are useful for quilting in straight lines or gentle curves and are ideal if you intend to quilt your project by the 'stitch in the ditch' method. The bar at the front of the foot has a central indentation, which can be lined up with your quilt seam making it easy to keep the stitching straight.

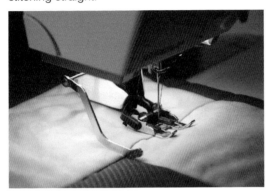

Walking feet can also be used with some fancy embroidery stitches provided the zig-zag throat plate is fitted to accommodate their width.

Stitch Length

I find machine quilting is more effective using a larger stitch length than for normal stitching. I usually turn my stitch length up to 3 or 3.5mm. This has the added advantage of being easier to unpick should you make a mistake.

Free-Motion Quilting

Free-motion quilting is essentially free-machine embroidery which is normally carried out on throws, quilts and larger items. For more details see the following technique.

Technique: Free-machine Embroidery   >

Handling Larger Quilts

If your quilting project is small, such as a lap or cot quilt, you may be able to manage, the portion, you are not stitching, by bunching it up loosely under the arm of the machine. If it is any larger, you will need to roll up the excess and feed it through the arm while you stitch.

Really large quilts may need to be rolled tightly and secured with special quilting clips (or those plastic-covered spring clips you use for hanging up garden tools in the shed). You may need a few strategically placed chairs in front of, and behind, your desk, to stop the weight of the rolled quilt dragging the whole lot onto the floor.

Free-machine Embroidery

Free-machine Embroidery is great for adding quick designs to all sorts of projects from bags to cushions to quilts.

What is Free-machine Embroidery?

Free-machine embroidery is stitching with the feed dogs (the little rows of serrated teeth under your presser foot) set to the down position and a darning or embroidery foot fitted. With the machine set up in this manner, you will find that you can stitch in any direction. You are completely in control of stitch width too, which is determined by how fast you run your machine and how fast you move your fabric. Free-machine embroidery is very rewarding, once you get the hang of it, although it does take a little practice.

The top tension of the machine is usually lowered to between 1-2 ½ but, with practice, you will find the ideal tension for your own machine.

Bobbin tension and threading for free-machine embroidery varies between different makes of machine and you should check the instruction manual for your particular model.

Free-machine embroidery can be carried out using a hoop, in which case you will only need your background fabric, or without a hoop. If you don't want to use a hoop, you will need to place a layer of batting and a layer of thin cotton backing behind your background fabric.

What Threads Should I Use?

As Free-machine embroidery is usually done for decorative purposes, I suggest you use a good quality machine embroidery thread on the top and toning all-purpose polyester on the bottom. If you are doing free-motion quilting, you could also consider using a good-quality cotton quilting thread on the top but still use a polyester on the bottom but one which matches your quilt backing.

Stitch Length

To achieve a consistent stitch length, it is important to run the sewing machine at a constant, fairly fast speed. If you can master this, all you then have to worry about is feeding your fabric through at an even rate without jerking or changing direction too suddenly. The only way to achieve this is practice, practice, practice until you can almost do it in your sleep (but please don't try this!). If you are lucky enough to own a machine that comes with a special stitch regulator foot, you will find the whole business a lot easier as the foot gauges the speed, at which you are moving the fabric, and regulates the motor speed accordingly.

Free-machine embroidery can be very tiring on the back and neck and you will need to take the occasional break. However, I find that wedging a hardback book, about 1cm thick, under the back edge of the machine, effectively tilting it towards you, makes the process a lot easier.

There are many stitches used in free-machine embroidery, but the most popular is stippling, which is very handy for filling in large areas of background. Stippling around an area of interest in your quilt can make it stand out more than usual.

89

Getting Started (With Hoop)

To get started in free-machine embroidery using a hoop:

1 Prepare your fabric by ironing thoroughly.

2 Place the inner ring of your embroidery hoop on a flat surface and lay your fabric on top, right side down, ensuring you cover the whole ring with at least 1" extra all round,

3 Place the outer ring over the inner ring and fabric and check the fabric is taut, but not stretched. Tighten the screw.

4 Turn the hoop over so when you place it under the needle the fabric will lie flat on the needle bed.

5 Thread up your machine according to the instruction manual, using machine embroidery thread on top and all-purpose polyester on the bobbin.

6 Fit your embroidery or darning foot if you have one and drop your feed dogs out of operation.

7 Adjust your top tension to 1 (this can be readjusted later on if you find it is too loose or tight).

8 Place your hoop under the presser foot. You may have to raise the foot a little higher to achieve this.

9 Lower the presser foot. Some darning or embroidery feet will not touch the fabric when lowered.

10 Take the end of the top thread in your left hand and hold it taut to the left of the needle bed.

11 Turn the machine handwheel towards you until the bottom thread comes up to the top of the fabric.

12 Take the ends of the top and bottom threads in your left hand and hold them taut to the left of the needle bed.

13 Now work a few stitches around the area where the bottom thread came through the fabric.

14 Snip off the ends of the top and bottom threads close to the fabric.

15 With your hands on either side of the hoop, stitch from side to side, in circles, curves or squares. Try writing your name or drawing a shape.

> **Note:**
> It is very important that you do not put your hands inside the embroidery hoop at any time while stitching. The needle will be moving very fast and you will be concentrating so hard that you may not notice your hand getting close to the needle until it is too late.

16 Try to run the machine at a constant speed at about half the rate the machine is capable of. At the same time, try and move the hoop at smoothly and evenly practising until you achieve an even stitch length.

17 Once you are happy with your stitching, fuse a shaped piece of fabric onto your background fabric and practise stitching round the edges.

18 You are now ready to attempt appliqué!

Getting Started (Without Hoop)

To get started in free-machine machine embroidery without using a hoop:

1 Place a layer of cotton batting, of the same size, behind your background fabric, followed by a layer of thin cotton or calico backing.

2 Press all three layers from the background fabric side.

3 Secure the layers together using quilters' safety pins randomly placed around the piece.

4 Continue from step 5 from the hoop instructions.

> **Note:**
> It is very important that you Hold your work by the edges when embroidering and do not put your hands anywhere near the needle or foot at any time while stitching. The needle will be moving very fast and you will be concentrating so hard that you may not notice your hand getting close to the needle until it is too late.

Part 4: What Next?

Moving on and tackling bigger, more complex projects.

More from Time4me Workshops

You can find more tips, techniques and videos at Margo Price's website.

Time4me-Workshops Website

The aim of my website is to promote traditional crafts by passing on knowledge, skills and experience to those who would like to learn about, or perhaps already enjoy, sewing.

In these pages you will find practical advice that will make your sewing projects easier and more enjoyable. You'll find advice on choosing and using wadding, getting started in dressmaking and top tips on appliqué.

Why not take a look at my videos on how to use men's shirts to make a traditional quilt? Or if cushion making is more your thing, there are a series of six videos showing you all you need to know.

To find out more, visit Margo Price's website at:

time4me-workshops.co.uk

How to Make a Living from Crafts

Using the craft of sewing as an example, this book will also provide essential reading for other craftsmen such as musicians, photographers, jewellery makers, card makers, knitters, woodworkers, gardeners, watercolour painters, clay modellers, mosaic artists, and many more.

This online e-book (also available in other formats) is suited to intermediate and advanced crafters who are producing work good enough to sell or who may be selling their wares already but are struggling to make a living. It also explains the benefits of branching out and teaching your skill to others and shows you how to set up and run your workshops.

To purchase this book, or find out more, visit Margo Price's website at:

time4me-workshops.co.uk

How to Get Started in Free-machine Embroidery

This book tells you all you need to know to get started in free machine embroidery.

It describes all the techniques and materials you'll need and gives tips for working in a safe and comfortable environment before moving on to describe five exciting ways to use free machine embroidery in a range of artistic projects.

This online e-book (available in various formats) is suitable for beginners or intermediates who want to be more creative in their sewing.

To purchase this book, or find out more, visit Margo Price's website at:

time4me-workshops.co.uk